I0605052

DAILY GRATITUDE

Publications International, Ltd.

Scripture quotations from *The Holy Bible, King James Version*

Images from Shutterstock.com

Louis Weber, CEO
Publications International, Ltd.
8140 Lehigh Avenue
Morton Grove, IL 60053

ISBN: 978-1-63938-866-0

Manufactured in China.

8 7 6 5 4 3 2 1

Table of Contents

Introduction

When we open our hearts to God, we see the ways his many blessings flow through us and imbue our lives with love and guidance. Sometimes, however, his grace is difficult to find. In times of doubt and anger, God seems distant from us. We become easily overwhelmed by our obligations, focusing on pain and hardship. Take comfort in your faith and remember that God will never abandon you. Find his loving presence all around you, in the ground beneath your feet, the warming sun on your face, and the gentle music of his songbirds.

Daily Gratitude is a daily guide to help refocus your faith as you express your feelings of thanks and appreciation toward God. Throughout this book, you'll find verses, reflections, poems, and prayers for every day of the year. Recognize that God is guiding you on your journey, and open your eyes to all he has to offer. Be thankful for his many blessings and welcome each and every day with a grateful heart.

Daily Gratitude

JANUARY

JANUARY 1

Ask, and it shall be given you; seek, and ye shall find; knock, and it shall be opened unto you: For every one that asketh receiveth; and he that seeketh findeth; and to him that knocketh it shall be opened.

—*MATTHEW 7:7–8*

LORD, throughout this year I want to explore your Word, appreciating the depth of your amazing love. I ask your blessings as I seek to deepen my relationship with you. Let me trust in your promise: that I need only to ask to receive. Thank you!

JANUARY 2

❝

A new heart also will I give you, and a new spirit will I put within you: and I will take away the stony heart out of your flesh, and I will give you an heart of flesh.

—EZEKIEL 36:26

FATHER, the start of a new year speaks of new opportunities. It is a good time to teach our children about forgiveness and the importance of trying again when we have failed.

We are thankful that you are a God of second chances. Just as you love us unconditionally, there is nothing our children could do to make us stop loving them. Help us teach them the hopeful message that there is no need for despair and that forgiveness and a new start are always possible.

JANUARY 3

“

And say ye, Save us, O God of our salvation, and gather us together, and deliver us from the heathen, that we may give thanks to thy holy name.

—1 CHRONICLES 16:35

THIS verse offers a short list of gifts from God: our salvation, our community, and our distinction as God’s children. Meditate on these gifts. Write down reasons to be grateful for them. Is there another blessing you would add to your list?

JANUARY 4

“

Wherefore we receiving a kingdom which cannot be moved, let us have grace, whereby we may serve God acceptably with reverence and godly fear.

—HEBREWS 12:28

LORD, help me serve you today with reverence. Earthly governments come and go, empires fail, but your kingdom cannot be shaken or moved. You are my King, and I'm grateful for your grace.

JANUARY 5

"

The King of love my shepherd is,
Whose goodness faileth never;
I nothing lack if I am his
And he is mine forever.

And so through all the length of days
Your goodness faileth never;
Good Shepherd, may I sing thy praise
Within thy house forever.

—Henry W. Baker

JANUARY 6

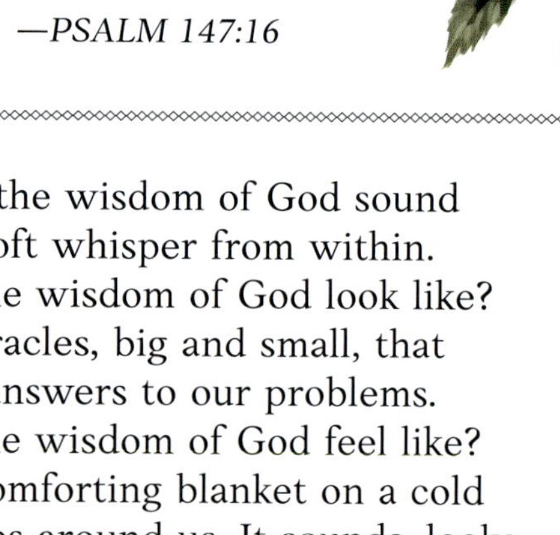

He giveth snow like wool: he scattereth the hoarfrost like ashes.

—PSALM 147:16

WHAT does the wisdom of God sound like? Like a soft whisper from within. What does the wisdom of God look like? Signs and miracles, big and small, that point to the answers to our problems. What does the wisdom of God feel like? Like a soft, comforting blanket on a cold day that wraps around us. It sounds, looks, and feels like love.

JANUARY 7

And let the peace of God rule in your hearts, to the which also ye are called in one body; and be ye thankful.

—*COLOSSIANS 3:15*

AS I let you rule in my heart today, Lord, give me your peace. I am confident in your calling me and in the unity I have with others in the faith. We are one body, and you are one Lord. Thank you for these gifts.

"For thou shalt eat the labour of thine hands: happy shalt thou be, and it shall be well with thee.

—PSALM 128:2

ALL work can be good, Lord, for you can upgrade the most mundane, difficult, or nerve-racking job into one that matters. God of all skills and vocations, bless and inspire my work.

JANUARY 9

"

And the Lord said unto Abram, after that Lot was separated from him, Lift up now thine eyes, and look from the place where thou art northward, and southward, and eastward, and westward: For all the land which thou seest, to thee will I give it, and to thy seed for ever.

—GENESIS 13:14–15

GOD gives because he is love. He gave the world and everything in it. When that was tossed aside, he redeemed mankind with another gift. It was the best he had to offer. The supreme gift. The total gift. In the person of his Son, he gave himself.

JANUARY 10

"

And at the dedication of the wall of Jerusalem they sought the Levites out of all their places, to bring them to Jerusalem, to keep the dedication with gladness, both with thanksgivings, and with singing.

—NEHEMIAH 12:27

AFTER the exile, Nehemiah rebuilt the walls of Jerusalem. Then he brought the people together to celebrate and dedicate themselves to the protection it represented. What wall of protection has God provided for you? Give thanks for his strength and generosity.

JANUARY 11

“For thou wilt light my candle: the Lord my God will enlighten my darkness.

—PSALM 18:28

GOD, your blessings abound. Even in the dark of winter, I see your hand in the beauty of frost on the windowpane, the kindness of the grocery clerk who helps an elderly woman load her purchases in her car, and the diligence of those who work at night to clear the roads. Even though it gets dark early these days, I see your light shining.

JANUARY 12

“

Saying, We give thee thanks, O Lord God Almighty, which art, and wast, and art to come; because thou hast taken to thee thy great power, and hast reigned.

—REVELATION 11:17

IN the end, Lord, I am most grateful for you, your constancy, and your majesty. I am grateful that you are my King today and that you always will be. Hear my prayer for your kingdom of peace and righteousness to flourish all across the glorious Earth, and thank you for all you have provided to me.

JANUARY 13

"

Be careful for nothing; but in every thing by prayer and supplication with thanksgiving let your requests be made known unto God.

—PHILIPPIANS 4:6

DO not be full of care today. Instead, take your cares to God in prayer, and do it with thanksgiving, feeling grateful that you can pray to him with an open heart and that he can provide for your needs.

JANUARY 14

“

Peace I leave with you, my peace I give unto you: not as the world giveth, give I unto you. Let not your heart be troubled, neither let it be afraid.

—JOHN 14:27

HOW restful it is to live in your love, Lord God! In the middle of chaos or turmoil, I remember that you are with me, and I am at peace once again. When it seems as if everything is falling apart, you hold me close in your love, and I am able to sleep at night. There is no other source of peace like belonging to you, Father.

JANUARY 15

And he dreamed, and behold a ladder set up on the earth, and the top of it reached to heaven: and behold the angels of God ascending and descending on it.

—GENESIS 28:12

GRATITUDE lifts us, like angels, above the cares that weigh us to the earth.

JANUARY 16

"

Thou wilt shew me the path of life: in thy presence is fulness of joy; at thy right hand there are pleasures for evermore.

—PSALM 16:11

THERE is joy in being in God's presence. There's no other place we find joy in its fullness, shimmering in all its facets, except in the presence of God himself. We can try manufacturing our own versions of joy by pursuing some of life's temporary pleasures—achievements, recreation, entertainment, material possessions, and such. But these don't come close to the rarified joy and gratitude we experience when we draw close to our heavenly Father.

JANUARY 17

“

This is the day which the Lord hath made; we will rejoice and be glad in it.

—PSALM 118:24

TODAY is the day you made, Lord. Please help to make me equal to its opportunities and challenges. Make me alert to your presence and power, and I will be grateful.

JANUARY 18

“That is, that I may be comforted together with you by the mutual faith both of you and me.

—ROMANS 1:12

BLESSED Creator, thank you for the loving people in my life. Thank you for their open hearts and minds. Thank you for making them like you. Amen.

JANUARY 19

"

I will praise thee, O Lord, with my whole heart; I will shew forth all thy marvellous works.

—PSALM 9:1

LORD, I want to praise you today, and I want to do it with my whole heart. Remind me of all your gracious works, and help me praise you for each of them. May your praise be on my lips all day as my heart overflows with thankfulness.

JANUARY 20

“

And the Lord shall scatter you among the nations, and ye shall be left few in number among the heathen, whither the Lord shall lead you.

—DEUTERONOMY 4:27

THANK you for our leaders. I might not always agree with them, but it is good to have people who will take charge and lead us. Help me remember to be thankful for those who dedicate their lives to public service, and help me to appreciate their vision of a brighter future.

JANUARY 21

He restoreth my soul: he leadeth me in the paths of righteousness for his name's sake.

—PSALM 23:3

GOD, you're leading me. With confidence I face my day. Every duty and interruption are appointments you've sent my way.

JANUARY 22

"

If ye then, being evil, know how to give good gifts unto your children: how much more shall your heavenly Father give the Holy Spirit to them that ask him?

—LUKE 11:13

FATHER, thank you for the gift of your Holy Spirit, who guides, protects, and gives solace. I dare to ask that you fill my soul and my life with the gift of your Spirit.

JANUARY 23

"

I know that thou canst do every thing, and that no thought can be withholden from thee.

—JOB 42:2

SOMETIMES it is so hard to take chances! Thank you, God, for giving me the courage to take a chance and try something new. I am so glad to be able to step out of my comfort zone and find the courage to change. What a gift to know that taking a chance could change my life! Thank you for the excitement of being brave.

"

The God of my rock; in him will I trust: he is my shield, and the horn of my salvation, my high tower, and my refuge, my saviour; thou savest me from violence. I will call on the Lord, who is worthy to be praised: so shall I be saved from mine enemies.

—2 SAMUEL 22:3–4

WE are grateful, O God, for glimpses we are given of you during times like these. Thank you for showing us how, during raging winds, the mother cardinal refuses to move, standing like a mighty shelter over the fledglings beneath her wings. Secure us in the truth that we, the children of your heart, are likewise watched over and protected during life's storms.

JANUARY 25

“

O give thanks unto the Lord; for he is good: for his mercy endureth for ever.

—PSALM 136:1

CONSIDER the goodness of God. The blessings you enjoy are not the result of our efforts but a reflection of God’s mercy. He is patient and kind, even when we don’t deserve it. Give thanks.

JANUARY 26

"

And the Word was made flesh, and dwelt among us, (and we beheld his glory, the glory as of the only begotten of the Father,) full of grace and truth.

—JOHN 1:14

SON of God, who came to Earth,
thank you for your love for us.
Son of Man, who dwelt among us,
thank you for your love for us.
Savior, who redeemed the world,
thank you for your love for us.
Jesus, living Word of God,
thank you for your love for us.

JANUARY 27

"

Lay not up for yourselves treasures upon earth, where moth and rust doth corrupt, and where thieves break through and steal: But lay up for yourselves treasures in heaven, where neither moth nor rust doth corrupt, and where thieves do not break through nor steal: For where your treasure is, there will your heart be also.

—*MATTHEW 6:19–21*

I asked for God's greatest riches, and he gave me contentment.

JANUARY 28

"

To the end that my glory may sing praise to thee, and not be silent. O Lord my God, I will give thanks unto thee for ever.

—PSALM 30:12

LORD, may I not be silent today. Help me, in song and word, to give thanks to you. As you reveal your glory in my life and ministry, I am grateful. Your kindness and mercy fills my heart until it overflows with joy.

JANUARY 29

“

That he would grant you, according to the riches of his glory, to be strengthened with might by his Spirit in the inner man.

—*EPHESIANS 3:16*

GOD, thank you for letting me cling to the faith that has sustained me through so much uncertainty and pain before. I now know that although faith may be all I have, it’s also all I need.

JANUARY 30

"

But a certain Samaritan, as he journeyed, came where he was: and when he saw him, he had compassion on him, And went to him, and bound up his wounds, pouring in oil and wine, and set him on his own beast, and brought him to an inn, and took care of him.

—LUKE 10:33–34

FATHER God, thank you for those angelic persons who bring healing. We will try to mimic their ways.

JANUARY 31

For there is hope of a tree, if it be cut down, that it will sprout again, and that the tender branch thereof will not cease.

—JOB 14:7

LORD, if we could see the future, it would be easy to have hope. Real hope is when we can't see the end of the road, but still trust you to lead us there.

Daily Gratitude

FEBRUARY

FEBRUARY 1

God is able to make all grace abound toward you; that ye, always having all sufficiency in all things, may abound to every good work.

—2 CORINTHIANS 9:8

WELL, it's a new month. We're in the dregs of winter, though, and it's hard to feel fresh and new. It's been gray and dreary outside, and the kids are bored and restless, tired of school and eager for spring sports to begin again.

Lord, I know you take us where we're at. Please give me the grace to see the blessings in the ordinary and humdrum. Thank you for the crises that aren't happening, the text from a friend with a funny joke, or my spouse taking the car in for an oil change. Bless my family, my friends, and the service workers I meet as I run my errands.

FEBRUARY 2

"

For every house is builded by some man; but he that built all things is God.

—HEBREWS 3:4

I am so grateful for my home! It may not be fancy, but it is my own place. How lucky I am to have a place to live safely. How good it is sometimes to retreat from the world and be alone with my things, my routines, and my space. Thank you, Lord, for giving me shelter and a place to call my own.

FEBRUARY 3

But now, O Lord, thou art our father; we are the clay, and thou our potter; and we all are the work of thy hand.

—ISAIAH 64:8

LORD, so often I believe I know exactly what I think and why, but then I sense your gentle nudging to look at the situation from your perspective. How generous of you to shine your wisdom into the dark corners of my heart and mind! Make me a believer wise in your ways—not one determined to have things my own way.

FEBRUARY 4

"

What things soever ye desire, when ye pray, believe that ye receive them, and ye shall have them.

—MARK 11:24

GIVE thanks and praise for what you have, and your prayers are already answered.

FEBRUARY 5

Every good gift and every perfect gift is from above, and cometh down from the Father of lights, with whom is no variableness, neither shadow of turning.

—JAMES 1:17

LORD, I'm grateful today for all your gifts, each of which is good and perfect. I'm even more grateful that you are unchangeable, providing a light without shadow. Guide my steps today and I will praise you.

FEBRUARY 6

“

He that receiveth you receiveth me, and he that receiveth me receiveth him that sent me. He that receiveth a prophet in the name of a prophet shall receive a prophet’s reward; and he that receiveth a righteous man in the name of a righteous man shall receive a righteous man’s reward.

—*MATTHEW 10:40–41*

A dedicated servant is grateful to all those who have served him, including the Lord. He sees that he is passing on to others what he has received.

FEBRUARY 7

The Lord is good, a strong hold in the day of trouble; and he knoweth them that trust in him.

—NAHUM 1:7

LORD, today I pray for all those who have sought all the wrong kinds of protection. It's so easy for us to become obsessed with protecting our marriages, our children, and our well-being to the extent that we are in danger of losing our peace of mind. Remind us all, Lord, that when we are in your hands, we are in the best of hands. You will never fail us. You will never renege on your promises. With you, we stand strong and have great hope.

"

[Jesus] had called the people unto him with his disciples also, he said unto them, Whosoever will come after me, let him deny himself, and take up his cross, and follow me . . . For what shall it profit a man, if he shall gain the whole world, and lose his own soul?

—*MARK 8:34, 36*

JESUS, your purposes are eternal ones, and they're generally the opposite of an earthbound here-and-now mindset. This verse makes it clear to me that it takes a committed heart and soul to follow you. So where I have become dusty or rusty in my attentiveness in following you, please come with the breath of your Spirit to refresh me and get me moving in your ways again.

FEBRUARY 9

But if we hope for that we see not, then do we with patience wait for it.

—ROMANS 8:25

IT is hard to be patient, but I am grateful for that gift. Whether it is waiting in line or anticipating a coming event, patience is a wonderful way to slow down and appreciate what is coming. Thank you for the gift of patience and the ability to take my time and savor every moment. Instead of saying, “I can’t wait!” I am happy to say, “I will wait my turn” as I anticipate what is to come.

FEBRUARY 10

"All things bright and beautiful,
All creatures great and small,
All things wise and wonderful,
The Lord God made them all.

—Cecil Frances Alexander

FEBRUARY 11

"

And God created great whales, and every living creature that moveth, which the waters brought forth abundantly, after their kind, and every winged fowl after his kind: and God saw that it was good.

—*GENESIS 1:21*

LORD, thank you for these angels who come to me in fluff and fur. Thank you for their magic of putting laughter in the hearts of those they love. Thank you for their trust and their unabashed desire to give affection and to be scratched behind the ears.

FEBRUARY 12

Whither shall I go from thy spirit? or whither shall I flee from thy presence?

—PSALM 139:7

LORD, you know me. Sometimes that thought is intimidating. I don't want you to see all my flaws and foibles! I become discouraged by the thought of how petty I must seem to you, how earthly my concerns. I think that if you truly know me, you'll think me unworthy of your love.

But I know you do love me! You alone can both fully know me and fully love me. I thank you for that incredible gift.

FEBRUARY 13

Lo, children are an heritage of the Lord; and the fruit of the womb is his reward.

—PSALM 127:3

HOW can I thank you enough for my spouse and children? When I step back from everyday concerns for a moment, I am overwhelmed with appreciation. We all have our flaws and sins, but you've given us a home full of love for each other. Please protect us from harm, guide us in your paths towards wisdom, and bless us abundantly.

FEBRUARY 14

Beloved, let us love one another: for love is of God; and every one that loveth is born of God, and knoweth God. He that loveth not knoweth not God; for God is love.

—1 JOHN 4:7–8

TODAY is Valentine's Day! While this holiday can be commercial, let me take it as an opportunity to thank you, God, for the people I love and the people who love me. I know all love ultimately flows from you, for you are love.

FEBRUARY 15

We are bound to thank God always for you, brethren, as it is meet, because that your faith groweth exceedingly, and the charity of every one of you all toward each other aboundeth.

—2 THESSALONIANS 1:3

THINK about a faithful friend today, someone who has loved you and God. This could be a parent, teacher, neighbor, or coworker. It could be a community, such as a group at church. Thank God for the people in your life who uplift you.

FEBRUARY 16

This also cometh forth from the Lord of hosts, which is wonderful in counsel, and excellent in working.

—ISAIAH 28:29

LORD, I looked at a recent problem from every angle imaginable, but it wasn't until I filtered it through your Word that the gems of wisdom and understanding appeared. How lost we would be without your guidance, Lord, and how blessed we are to have your counsel.

FEBRUARY 15

“

We are bound to thank God always for you, brethren, as it is meet, because that your faith groweth exceedingly, and the charity of every one of you all toward each other aboundeth.

—2 THESSALONIANS 1:3

THINK about a faithful friend today, someone who has loved you and God. This could be a parent, teacher, neighbor, or coworker. It could be a community, such as a group at church. Thank God for the people in your life who uplift you.

FEBRUARY 16

This also cometh forth from the Lord of hosts, which is wonderful in counsel, and excellent in working.

—ISAIAH 28:29

LORD, I looked at a recent problem from every angle imaginable, but it wasn't until I filtered it through your Word that the gems of wisdom and understanding appeared. How lost we would be without your guidance, Lord, and how blessed we are to have your counsel.

FEBRUARY 17

He shall give his angels charge over thee, to keep thee.

—LUKE 4:10

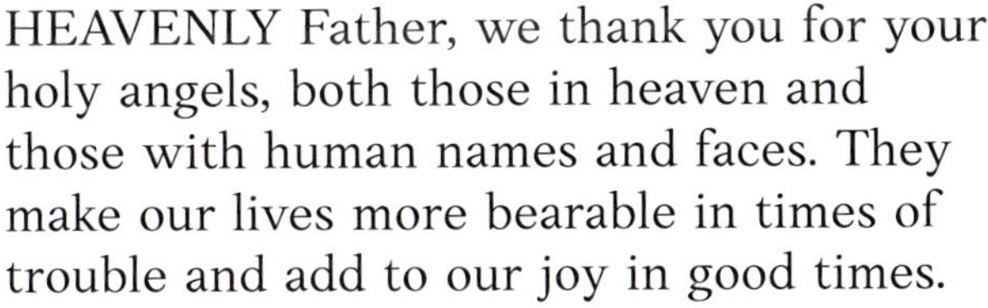

HEAVENLY Father, we thank you for your holy angels, both those in heaven and those with human names and faces. They make our lives more bearable in times of trouble and add to our joy in good times.

Keep us always in your sight, Lord. When we stumble, please send your merciful messengers to pick us up again. When we are lost, send them to light the way home.

FEBRUARY 18

If thine enemy be hungry, give him bread to eat; and if he be thirsty, give him water to drink.

—PROVERBS 25:21

SERVING others is the foundation of true gratitude.

FEBRUARY 19

"Not by works of righteousness which we have done, but according to his mercy he saved us, by the washing of regeneration, and renewing of the Holy Ghost.

—TITUS 3:5

LORD, I am grateful that you don't have a list of criteria for being eligible for salvation. What insecurity that would create in us! I feel blessed that I don't need to resort to servile fear or self-important boasting when it comes to my standing with you. Your salvation is a gift available to all and secured by your merits—not mine. It is received only by grace through faith in you.

FEBRUARY 20

The just man walketh in his integrity: his children are blessed after him.

—PROVERBS 20:7

I feel your hand on mine as I learn to be a good parent, O God, knowing that together you and I are instilling lifelong values and beliefs. I wish it were a straight-lined experience, but for me, it is more like a zigzag, making my growth seem slow. And yet I am grateful for all the help you give.

FEBRUARY 21

Well done, good and faithful servant; thou hast been faithful over a few things, I will make thee ruler over many things: enter thou into the joy of thy Lord.

—MATTHEW 25:23

BLESSINGS, like miracles, appear only when we believe in them. Faith gives us the eyes with which to see and to believe what we see.

FEBRUARY 22

Let your light so shine before men, that they may see your good works, and glorify your Father which is in heaven.

—MATTHEW 5:16

GOD, thank you for giving me this light of mine to shine. I promise never to conceal the brilliance you've bestowed upon me. May I forever reflect the glow of your loving presence.

FEBRUARY 23

I will bless the Lord at all times: his praise shall continually be in my mouth.

—PSALM 34:1

TODAY, Lord, help me to be grateful at all times. During every meal and kind encounter with a stranger, at every glimpse of your generosity or evidence of your presence, give me words to praise you, out loud and in my heart. Amen.

FEBRUARY 24

Confess your faults one to another, and pray one for another, that ye may be healed. The effectual fervent prayer of a righteous man availeth much.

—JAMES 5:16

LORD, if all the prayers ever prayed were linked together, surely they would reach to heaven and back countless times! We want to be a people who pray without ceasing, Lord. Hear both the prayers we utter and the silent prayers of our hearts, and may you also sense how grateful we are to serve a God who listens to our prayers and sends us his answers.

FEBRUARY 25

And all things, whatsoever ye shall ask in prayer, believing, ye shall receive.

—MATTHEW 21:22

LORD, thank you for always listening to my concerns. So often I begin praying in one direction only to sense you turning my thoughts around until I end up praying for something quite different. Only later do I realize you were gently guiding me in a better direction. What blessed communication! I am so grateful.

FEBRUARY 26

O give thanks unto the Lord; for he is good; for his mercy endureth for ever.

—1 CHRONICLES 16:34

OF all the things for which we should be grateful, God's mercy should be chief. He does not give us what we deserve, he gives us his grace and forgiveness forever. Give thanks!

FEBRUARY 27

For I was an hungred, and ye gave me meat: I was thirsty, and ye gave me drink: I was a stranger, and ye took me in: Naked, and ye clothed me: I was sick, and ye visited me.

—MATTHEW 25:35–36

WHEN I don't feel well, it is easy to feel sorry for myself. Then I remember the people who support me and help me when I am unwell. Thank you for the friends and family, the neighbors and coworkers, the nurses and doctors, and everyone else who goes out of the way to brighten my day and make me see a ray of light in the darkness.

FEBRUARY 28

The heavens declare the glory of God; and the firmament sheweth his handywork.

—PSALM 19:1

WINTERS can be long, Lord, as I've complained before, and hope elusive. Thank you for sending me outdoors. My spirit soars at the sight of a woodchuck waking from winter sleep. I rub sleep from my eyes, grateful for signposts of change, like paw prints in the mud, leading me to springs of the soul.

FEBRUARY 29

“

Open thou mine eyes, that I may behold wondrous things out of thy law.

—PSALM 119:18

LORD, thank you for this Leap Day! Let me treat this not just as any other day but as a special gift. I ask that you open my eyes to all the instances of grace around me. Let me take a special delight in the splendor of your creation. Let me see the best in people today.

Daily Gratitude
MARCH

MARCH 1

God of the granite and the rose,
Soul of the sparrow and the bee,
The mighty tide of being flows,
Thro' countless channels, Lord, from Thee.

—Elizabeth Doten

MARCH 2

For which cause we faint not; but though our outward man perish, yet the inward man is renewed day by day.

—2 CORINTHIANS 4:16

FINALLY I've emerged from the dark night into the light with new energy, renewed vigor, and a body that responds again. Thank you for recovery and wholeness. And bless me as I tell others how good you are!

MARCH 3

Sing unto the Lord, bless his name; shew forth his salvation from day to day.

—PSALM 96:2

THE word sing appears about 150 times in the Bible. It must be important to give praise to God in song. Ask our Father to put a song in your heart or even on your lips today. God is good, and for that we must spread gratitude.

MARCH 4

Be strong and of a good courage; be not afraid, neither be thou dismayed: for the Lord thy God is with thee whithersoever thou goest.

—JOSHUA 1:9

LORD, what a relief it is to know that whether I'm going to the corner grocery for milk and eggs or on a trip via a plane, train, or car, you are with me. You never have a scheduling conflict, and you are more necessary than my car keys or a boarding pass. Thank you for always coming with me, Lord. Some days I could hardly take a step outside my house without leaning on you.

MARCH 5

Finally, brethren, whatsoever things are true, whatsoever things are honest, whatsoever things are just, whatsoever things are pure, whatsoever things are lovely, whatsoever things are of good report; if there be any virtue, and if there be any praise, think on these things.

—PHILIPPIANS 4:8

THANK you, Lord, for the hobbies that I enjoy. How much joy I get out of these pleasures! Thank you for the chance to create, play, and enjoy. I am grateful for the people who share my hobby and who have become my friends. What a gift to share the joy of our pastimes together!

MARCH 6

Why take ye thought for raiment? Consider the lilies of the field, how they grow; they toil not, neither do they spin: And yet I say unto you, That even Solomon in all his glory was not arrayed like one of these.

—MATTHEW 6:28–29

LORD, how freeing it is to rid our drawers and closets of unneeded clothing and pass it along to someone who can really use it! Thanks for reminding us that since you provide for our needs, we don't need to hold on to any surplus. Keep us mindful that true beauty comes not from the latest fashions but from hearts dedicated to sharing your love with the world.

MARCH 7

"

Let thy tender mercies come unto me, that I may live: for thy law is my delight.

—PSALM 119:77

HEAVENLY Father, it is good to remember that everything that lives and breathes is sacred to you. We must never feel superior to any other human being—for we are all precious in your eyes. You have given us life, and we must make the choices that lead to kindness and peace. You created us, but how we live together is up to us. Thank you.

MARCH 8

The wind bloweth where it listeth, and thou hearest the sound thereof, but canst not tell whence it cometh, and whither it goeth: so is every one that is born of the Spirit.

—JOHN 3:8

LISTEN to the wind! I am thankful for its power. The wind is a gift that freshens the air and scrubs it clean. Without the wind, our weather would never change. Thank you, God, for the blessing of the wind and the power it has to change our world and make all things fresh and new.

MARCH 9

For we are labourers together with God: ye are God's husbandry, ye are God's building.

—1 CORINTHIANS 3:9

LORD, I look around at work and think how wonderful it is that so many different people can become a team. Thank you for my coworkers and supervisors. We may have our differences and challenging moments, but it is good to know that we are all working together toward a common goal. Thank you for the friendships I develop with my coworkers and for bringing us together in a special place.

MARCH 10

Bear ye one another's burdens, and so fulfil the law of Christ.

—GALATIANS 6:2

THANK you, Lord, for helping us through our hard times. You have shown your love for us and made us more compassionate people. Help us show the same love to others who are facing struggles.

MARCH 11

O come, let us sing unto the Lord: let us make a joyful noise to the rock of our salvation.

—PSALM 95:1

YOU may not be an opera star or a recording artist, but you can make a joyful noise. May your day be filled with laughter and praise as you ground yourself in the salvation of God.

MARCH 12

I know thy works: behold, I have set before thee an open door, and no man can shut it: for thou hast a little strength, and hast kept my word, and hast not denied my name.

—REVELATION 3:8

AN open door is an invitation. Just as the gates of heaven are open to all who follow God's will, an open door invites me in to experience new joys and revelations. Thank you, God, for allowing me to see the open doors in my life and take advantage of new experiences. Let me walk through them with Jesus at my side.

MARCH 13

Always in every prayer of mine for you all making request with joy.

—PHILIPPIANS 1:4

AS you think of your friends and family today, pray for them and thank God for them. Fill your day with intentional and joyful prayer, mindfully and gratefully remembering the people you love.

MARCH 14

A faithful man shall abound with blessings: but he that maketh haste to be rich shall not be innocent.

—PROVERBS 28:20

RATHER than proudly striving to get ahead on our own, we must learn to relax in the provision God has made for us. Only this will bring us God's peaceful rest.

MARCH 15

I will praise the name of God with a song, and will magnify him with thanksgiving.

—PSALM 69:30

THINK of a song you know, a worship song or hymn from church. How does this song bring you closer to God? Look up the words. Read all the verses. Hum the tune, and feel God's love reverberate through you. It is good to praise the name of God with a song.

MARCH 16

For the Lord giveth wisdom: out of his mouth cometh knowledge and understanding.

—PROVERBS 2:6

WHAT a blessing to have a second chance! Grant me the wisdom to use this opportunity wisely. And save me from the fear that I'll fall into the same old traps as last time. This is a brand new day, a whole new beginning.

MARCH 17

As many as are led by the Spirit of God, they are the sons of God.

—*ROMANS 8:14*

GOD, I am a child no longer, yet I still know the need to have someone take me by the hand and lead me out of this scary place. Throughout my life you've sent those people to me, and together we have found the way. Bless those angels, Lord. May they find the hands to hold when they need them. Amen.

MARCH 18

O bless our God, ye people, and make the voice of his praise to be heard.

—PSALM 66:8

THIS is my prayer today, Lord: that my praise will be heard, by you and those I love. Help me be outspoken in my gratitude so others will join me in a chorus of praise.

MARCH 19

The voice of joy, and the voice of gladness, the voice of the bridegroom, and the voice of the bride, the voice of them that shall say, Praise the Lord of hosts: for the Lord is good; for his mercy endureth for ever.

—JEREMIAH 33:11

A wedding is a fountain of joy for the bride and bridegroom. They are delighted in each other—you can see it on their faces and hear it in their voices. Thank God today for the love and joy he blesses us with in our loved ones and families.

MARCH 20

Ye that fear the Lord, praise him; all ye the seed of Jacob, glorify him; and fear him, all ye the seed of Israel.

—PSALM 22:23

PROPERLY understood, the fear of the Lord is reverence and awe, not a destabilizing anxiety. It is the knowledge that he is powerful and righteous. We can be grateful that the Lord is watching over us and blessing us.

MARCH 21

Then shalt thou walk in thy way safely, and thy foot shall not stumble.

—PROVERBS 3:23

TODAY my mind is thinking of places far away from me. I am grateful for the places I have traveled to and the opportunity to see new things and meet new people. I am grateful for the places I haven't seen and the anticipation and promise of trips to come. Thank you, Lord, for making it possible for me to leave my surroundings and visit new places.

MARCH 22

The Lord is my strength and my shield; my heart trusted in him, and I am helped: therefore my heart greatly rejoiceth; and with my song will I praise him.

—PSALM 28:7

THE Lord is your protector and helper; he is at once your strength and your shield. Take a moment to remind yourself that you can trust in him today. It's enough to make you want to sing hallelujah from a grateful heart.

MARCH 23

John answered and said, A man can receive nothing, except it be given him from heaven.

—JOHN 3:27

THERE is no such thing as a self-made man or woman. Everything is a gift, for which we rightly thank God. Gratitude is the only appropriate response to a generous and gracious God.

MARCH 24

For it is God which worketh in you both to will and to do of his good pleasure.

—PHILIPPIANS 2:13

HAVING faith is believing that even small things have significance. People of faith believe that every person matters, even one person can make a difference, and that God takes small things and makes them into great things.

MARCH 25

Rejoice in the Lord, O ye righteous: for praise is comely for the upright.

—PSALM 33:1

HOW might praise make you more attractive? Because a grateful heart lends itself to a joyful countenance, and all God's faithful children love a genuine smile. So rejoice in the Lord, for praise is comely for the upright.

MARCH 26

As ye have therefore received Christ Jesus the Lord, so walk ye in him: Rooted and built up in him, and stablished in the faith, as ye have been taught, abounding therein with thanksgiving.

—COLOSSIANS 2:6–7

JESUS was the fulfillment of God's promise of salvation. His life and death made salvation possible for us. What a glorious, selfless gift! I ponder this blessing every day, and gratitude and joy fill my very being.

MARCH 27

And God saw the light, that it was good: and God divided the light from the darkness.

—GENESIS 1:4

I am feeling my way in this darkness, God, and it seems I'm going in circles. Yet you have reminded me—quietly, just now—that encircled by your love with every move in any direction I go no closer to you—nor farther either—than already centered I am.

MARCH 28

The Lord is far from the wicked: but he heareth the prayer of the righteous.

—PROVERBS 15:29

O Lord, please help me to understand that I won't always get what I pray for. In the same regard, I want to learn to thank you more for everything you do give me. Amen.

MARCH 29

He sendeth the springs into the valleys, which run among the hills.

—PSALM 104:10

THE older I get, the more aware I am of the seasons of life, Lord. I know that when we draw our energy and resources from your living Word, we truly can be compared to the trees that thrive near streams of water. The fruit of a young life lived for you may look a bit different than the fruit visible in the lives of older folks, but it all brings you glory. Thank you, Lord, for supplying your living water through all the seasons of our lives. Without it, we could bear no worthy fruit.

Let not mercy and truth forsake thee: bind them about thy neck; write them upon the table of thine heart.

—*PROVERBS 3:3*

FAITH in God's love frees me to be the real me, for I remember that God sees me as I am and loves me with all his heart.

MARCH 31

And Jesus answered and said unto him, What wilt thou that I should do unto thee? The blind man said unto him, Lord, that I might receive my sight. And Jesus said unto him, Go thy way; thy faith hath made thee whole. And immediately he received his sight, and followed Jesus in the way.

—MARK 10:51–52

THANK God when the pain ends, when once again we're well and whole and strong. Thank God when our bodies are released from the blinding, mind-numbing hurts that affect our whole lives. Thank God when we have complete victory over pain.

Daily Gratitude

APRIL

APRIL 1

“

And in that day shall ye say, Praise the Lord, call upon his name, declare his doings among the people, make mention that his name is exalted.

—ISAIAH 12:4

LORD, this is that day—the day I praise you, pray to you, and talk about you. Help me mention your name to family and friends and do so with reverence and joy. Help me to exalt your name.

APRIL 2

Blessed be the God and Father of our Lord Jesus Christ, who hath blessed us with all spiritual blessings in heavenly places in Christ.

—EPHESIANS 1:3

LORD, no matter what we bring of ourselves to give you, even if we include all our hopes and dreams, it's never enough to give in return for all you've given to us. And so we give you our praise. We sing to you and come before you with our meager offerings, praying all the while that you will make something marvelous of them.

APRIL 3

Call unto me, and I will answer thee, and show thee great and mighty things, which thou knowest not.

—JEREMIAH 33:3

O God, instill in my children the heart of an adventurer off to explore every corner of your marvelous creation and to find their place in it. Thank you for blessing the quest and relieving my anxiety by promising to be a part of their journey step by step.

APRIL 4

Yea, though I walk through the valley of the shadow of death, I will fear no evil: for thou art with me; thy rod and thy staff they comfort me.

—PSALM 23:4

MANY times I feel that I have the right to be downcast. But God's Word says that we should not be downcast because we have an amazing hope through him. If I focus on this hope, joy will enter my spirit, and my negative emotions will disperse.

APRIL 5

We believe that through the grace of the Lord Jesus Christ we shall be saved.

—ACTS 15:11

LORD Jesus Christ, how grateful I am that—because of your grace and not because of my own words or deeds—you have cleansed me of my sins and offered me the gifts of forgiveness and salvation with open arms. What glorious, selfless gifts! Thank you for opening up the way for me to enjoy eternal life with you. I am saved only by grace through faith in you.

APRIL 6

Praise ye the Lord. O give thanks unto the Lord; for he is good: for his mercy endureth.

—PSALM 106:1

OVER and over scripture reminds us of God's mercy and goodness, both aspects of his love. Together they represent blessings we receive in abundance. For this, we praise him and give thanks.

APRIL 7

Lord, thou hast heard the desire of the humble: thou wilt prepare their heart, thou wilt cause thine ear to hear: To judge the fatherless and the oppressed, that the man of the earth may no more oppress.

—PSALM 10:17–18

LORD, today I ask you to slow me down and open my ears so I will notice the needs of those around me. Too often I breeze by people with an offhand greeting but remain in a cocoon of my own concerns. I know many around me are hurting, Lord. Help me find ways to be of service.

APRIL 8

The earth is the Lord's, and the fulness thereof; the world, and they that dwell therein.

—PSALM 24:1

THE trees are just beginning to bud, and my neighbor's daffodils are brightening the view. Thank you for spring, God, for new beginnings. I marvel in the beauty of your creation, the intricacies of your designs. I ask that you keep my eyes open to the wonders of nature.

APRIL 9

For the Lord shall comfort Zion: he will comfort all her waste places; and he will make her wilderness like Eden, and her desert like the garden of the Lord; joy and gladness shall be found therein, thanksgiving, and the voice of melody.

—ISAIAH 51:3

LORD, comfort me today. Turn the barrenness I feel into gardens of delight. Give me joy and gladness. Give me glorious music and a thankful heart. You promise to comfort your people, and I need your comfort today.

APRIL 10

Be strong and of a good courage, fear not, nor be afraid of them: for the Lord thy God, he it is that doth go with thee; he will not fail thee, nor forsake thee.

—DEUTERONOMY 31:6

GOD, bless those angels who shake hands with danger on a daily basis. Help them know that their efforts are not only noticed but appreciated. Give them courage with caution. Give them life with meaning. Give them the strength to withstand the pressure and risk.

APRIL 11

The memory of the just is blessed: but the name of the wicked shall rot.

—PROVERBS 10:7

THANK you for the gift of memory. Playing "I remember" is such fun, Lord of history, especially the sharing of it with children and grandchildren who, like relay runners, are here to pick up their part of our family tale.

APRIL 12

For every creature of God is good, and nothing to be refused, if it be received with thanksgiving: For it is sanctified by the word of God and prayer.

—1 TIMOTHY 4:4–5

PAUL is talking about meat here, releasing Timothy from strict dietary restrictions. But everything and everyone God created can be received with thanksgiving, made pure by God's promises and our prayer. Spend the day prayerfully thanking him for the people and things around you.

APRIL 13

He hath made the earth by his power, he hath established the world by his wisdom, and hath stretched out the heavens by his discretion.

—JEREMIAH 10:12

TO embrace the gifts each day brings is to acknowledge that the Creator never walks away from his creation. Rather, his hand is always at work making us better than we know we can bc.

APRIL 14

Thank you for both rain and sun.
Thank you for both night and day.
Thank you for both quiet and noise.
Thank you for both challenges
And for peaceful times.
Thank you when I have little,
And thank you when I have much.
Thank you in all times.

APRIL 15

“

The light of the eyes rejoiceth the heart.

—PROVERBS 15:30

WHEN you look around today, know the blessing of seeing God in every smiling face. Reflect that blessing in your own eyes, quietly and with a kind heart.

APRIL 16

Now therefore, our God, we thank thee, and praise thy glorious name.

—1 CHRONICLES 29:13

LORD, how important it is for us to be thankful at all times. It's so easy to fall into the trap of having specific expectations and then despairing when events take an unexpected turn. You are working in our lives every moment, Lord. We will do our part by working hard and taking full advantage of all opportunities that come our way, but we also know that some matters are reserved for you. We are thankful that nothing is beyond your control, Lord, and we are grateful that you are our wise leader.

APRIL 17

Wherefore receive ye one another, as Christ also received us to the glory of God.

—ROMANS 15:7

LORD, how grateful I am for the gift of hospitality. When others make me feel welcome in their homes, it fills me with warmth and love. Help me to cultivate this gift in myself, Lord, so that those who enter my home may find sweet joy, comfort, and hope.

APRIL 18

He healeth the broken in heart, and bindeth up their wounds.

—PSALM 147:3

THANK you, Lord, for enduring unimaginable pain, even to the point of death, so that my broken relationship with my heavenly Father can be healed. By that healing, may all my emotional wounds be healed as well. In your name I pray. Amen.

APRIL 19

I will mention the lovingkindnesses of the Lord, and the praises of the Lord, according to all that the Lord hath bestowed on us.

—*ISAIAH 63:7*

GOD, help me mention your love today. I want to praise you to my friends and family, being conscious of all you have given me and reminding everyone of how great you are.

APRIL 20

“Moreover, brethren, I declare unto you the gospel which I preached unto you, which also ye have received, and wherein ye stand; By which also ye are saved, if ye keep in memory what I preached unto you, unless ye have believed in vain. For I delivered unto you first of all that which I also received, how that Christ died for our sins according to the scriptures.

—1 CORINTHIANS 15:1–3

LIVING God, we sing for joy as we remember the resurrection of your son, Jesus. Because he died and rose again, our hopes for paradise are real. Because he lives, we live. Fill us with wonder as together our family contemplates the awesome mystery of the cross. Accept our praises and our songs of gratitude.

APRIL 21

But they that wait upon the Lord shall renew their strength; they shall mount up with wings as eagles; they shall run, and not be weary; and they shall walk, and not faint.

—ISAIAH 40:31

I see a robin's egg hatching, Lord, and am set free from my doubts and fretting. While life is not always filled with joy and happiness, I know it is always held in your hand.

APRIL 22

Now therefore, if ye will obey my voice indeed, and keep my covenant, then ye shall be a peculiar treasure unto me above all people: for all the earth is mine.

—EXODUS 19:5

O God, giver of all good things, our faith in you is like a treasure to be mined—it sustains, it inspires, and it provides us with unimagined contentment.

APRIL 23

Lord, since you exist, we exist.
Since you are beautiful,
we are beautiful.
Since you are good, we are good.
By our existence we honour you.
By our beauty we glorify you.
By our goodness we love you.

—Edmund of Abingdon

APRIL 24

And all the people came up after him, and the people piped with pipes, and rejoiced with great joy, so that the earth rent with the sound of them.

—1 KINGS 1:40

GO forth in the joy of the Lord, knowing how blessed you are.

APRIL 25

I will praise thee; for I am fearfully and wonderfully made: marvellous are thy works; and that my soul knoweth right well.

—PSALM 139:14

RUNNING is so good. Can muscles silently praise you, God? I catch a vision of life's goodness in the pounding of my feet, even in the sweat pouring down. You made this warm machine, and you gave me the responsibility to keep it going. I will pray now with energy and exertion. But I will not pray with words for awhile for you are here as I pick up speed. And what, after all, needs to be said aloud at this moment?

APRIL 26

But seek ye first the kingdom of God, and his righteousness; and all these things shall be added unto you.

—MATTHEW 6:33

WE want it all and we want it now. But God knows better what is ours, and when we should have it. Relax and stop trying so hard! Let life flow and have faith that what is needed will arrive in good measure at just the right time.

APRIL 27

Behold, I will make thee a new sharp threshing instrument having teeth: thou shalt thresh the mountains, and beat them small, and shalt make the hills as chaff.

—ISAIAH 41:15

BLESS these tools of my work, Lord. Keep them sharp and strong and ready to do my will. And bless these hands, too, that they might be ready to do all you desire.

APRIL 28

And this commandment have we from him, That he who loveth God love his brother also.

—1 JOHN 4:21

LORD, it is sometimes hard to love those around me when they are so different in their beliefs and behaviors. I find myself sometimes feeling intolerant, even afraid. But you gave me the commandment to love others as myself, and that if I love you, then I love all of your creation.

Help me open my heart and mind to those I see as different, and find in them the common light of your presence. Help me be a better person and not fear others just because they are not like me. Help me see the wonder and magic in learning about others and letting them learn about me.

APRIL 29

Ointment and perfume rejoice the heart: so doth the sweetness of a man's friend by hearty counsel.

—PROVERBS 27:9

GOD, encouragement through friends and family lifts my heart just as sunshine turns roses skyward. May their love inspire me to stretch my soul toward the warmth and nurture of your radiant affection for me.

APRIL 30

Now the Lord is that Spirit: and where the Spirit of the Lord is, there is liberty.

—2 CORINTHIANS 3:17

LORD, how blessed we are to live in a country where we are free to worship as we please. Help us to never take such freedom for granted. Today we ask you to bless any believers who are being persecuted for living out their faith. Draw especially near to them, Lord. Surround them with your mighty army of angels.

Daily Gratitude

MAY

MAY 1

This book of the law shall not depart out of thy mouth; but thou shalt meditate therein day and night, that thou mayest observe to do according to all that is written therein: for then thou shalt make thy way prosperous, and then thou shalt have good success.

—JOSHUA 1:8

LORD, focusing on your Word is a great blessing. The more I keep it before me, the more faithfully I walk in your ways. Help me to make the most of every opportunity I have to read, think about, and discuss the things you share with us through the scriptures.

MAY 2

Rejoice in the Lord always: and again I say, Rejoice.

—*PHILIPPIANS 4:4*

THANK you, O God, for those moments of indescribable joy that surprise, that greet me unexpectedly in a child's hug, a drawing, a conversation, an uncontrollable giggle, and most especially an openness that not only lets me into their lives but draws me in.

MAY 3

Lord, you gave me a great team of helpers,
And for that I'm exceedingly thankful.
Where would I be without them?
They seem to know my needs before I do,
And they jump to meet them.
I know you've given them those gifts of caring,
Of encouragement, of hospitality and healing,
And they're using those gifts as you intended,
To show your love to others, including me.
I am thankful to you and to them.
I may be unable to repay them, Lord.
They'd probably refuse a reward anyway.
So I ask you to shower them with blessings,
Just as they have brought blessings to me.
Give them joy and peace in rich supply,
And let your love continue to flow
To them, within them, and through them.
Amen.

MAY 4

"

I know that, whatsoever God doeth, it shall be for ever: nothing can be put to it, nor any thing taken from it.

—ECCLESIASTES 3:14

LORD, in a world where everything seems to be here today and gone tomorrow, how wonderful it is to focus on the rich legacy we have in you. Everything you do and create lasts forever. How reassuring it is to accept that that means we will last forever too in your kingdom. Thank you, Lord.

MAY 5

"

Let us come before his presence with thanksgiving, and make a joyful noise unto him with psalms.

—PSALM 95:2

FATHER, help me make joyful noises today. Perhaps a sigh of satisfaction, or a simple thank you to a friend. Perhaps it is a full-throated song of praise driving alone in the car. May I speak to you clearly and with gratitude, knowing I am surrounded by your presence.

MAY 6

"

The Lord will give strength unto his people; the Lord will bless his people with peace.

—PSALM 29:11

LORD, it's hard to be grateful for difficult times. Help me to see my trials as an opportunity to grow and change. Help me reach out to others who are suffering their own difficult times. Thank you, God, for the chance to know you better through my suffering. Help me remember and be grateful for the suffering you endured to help me. Let me find the bright side of every trial and the strength to be grateful for the test.

MAY 7

"And be ye kind one to another, tenderhearted, forgiving one another, even as God for Christ's sake hath forgiven you.

—EPHESIANS 4:32

LORD, why is it that we see the faults of others so clearly but ignore our own until the pile gets so big, we finally trip over it? We desire to be more gracious than we are, Lord. Just as you have showered us with kindness and forgiveness, help us to do the same for those around us. Speak to our hearts, Lord. Open them and fill them with compassion.

MAY 8

The name of the Lord is a strong tower: the righteous runneth into it, and is safe.

—PROVERBS 18:10

HOW exciting it is to see and hear the busy hum of a city! I am thankful for all the people who live and work in cities. They have created places that thrum with life and energy. Great things can come from that energy, and I am grateful for the experiences cities provide to all of us.

MAY 9

"I am come that they might have life, and that they might have it more abundantly.

—JOHN 10:10

LORD, sometimes I feel like we are all only living out a minuscule amount of the life you have offered us. Help us tap into your stream of living water on a regular basis. Teach us to live more courageously, love more extravagantly, and give more generously. We don't want life to pass us by. Keep us open to all you have wrapped up in this gift called life. And then one day, bring us into abundant life with you.

MAY 10

“

Her children arise up, and call her blessed; her husband also, and he praiseth her.

—PROVERBS 31:28

MOMS are like flowers: Some are bright and showy, others simple and elegant. But all moms are beautiful, their faces turned toward the sun to reflect the light of the loving God that made them bloom.

MAY 11

“

Strength and honour are her clothing; and she shall rejoice in time to come. She openeth her mouth with wisdom; and in her tongue is the law of kindness.

—PROVERBS 31:25–26

BEING a mother may be the biggest challenge I’ve ever undertaken, but it’s taught me that I am so much more capable than I ever knew. With faith in God and belief in myself, I can accomplish anything.

MAY 12

And let us not be weary in well doing: for in due season we shall reap, if we faint not.

—GALATIANS 6:9

OVER and over I ask myself, "What can I do? What can I do to make a difference?" One of the hardest things about reaching out is having others think I can "fix it" and then finding out that I can't. Lord, help me to remember that what you promise is not to "fix it" for us but rather to give us whatever it takes to prevail in spite of our hurts. Help me keep in mind that sometimes all that is necessary is a listening ear.

MAY 13

"

The Lord hath appeared of old unto me, saying, Yea, I have loved thee with an everlasting love: therefore with lovingkindness have I drawn thee.

—JEREMIAH 31:3

LORD, please bring this truth home to my heart today: that the essence of God is love—your love reaching us and setting our hearts aglow with love for you and for all people. Let love rule this day. Let love rule my heart. Help me enjoy living successfully in your wonderful love.

MAY 14

“

And Jesus went forth, and saw a great multitude, and was moved with compassion toward them, and he healed their sick.

—MATTHEW 14:14

BEING ill lately has been difficult—having to accept help from others all the time! But you have shown me, Lord, that unless I am open to others’ gifts, I deprive them of all the pleasure of offering.

MAY 15

“

I will also praise thee with the psaltery, even thy truth, O my God: unto thee will I sing with the harp, O thou Holy One of Israel.

—PSALM 71:22

I might not be able to praise you with an instrument, Lord, but I can still thank you for your faithfulness.

When I’m folding laundry, I can praise you for the clothes on my back. When I’m stuck in traffic, I can praise you for the beautiful scenery surrounding me. When I’m fighting an illness, I can praise you for the Spirit you breathed into me. And when the people I love struggle, I can praise you for bringing such wonderful people into my life.

MAY 16

But ye, beloved, building up yourselves on your most holy faith, praying in the Holy Ghost, Keep yourselves in the love of God, looking for the mercy of our Lord Jesus Christ unto eternal life.

—JUDE 1:20–21

THIS gift of life is precious, and I know my eternity is secure in you. Though my days are not always easy, I know that you stay faithfully by my side, guiding my steps and filling my heart with joy.

I praise you with all the resources at my disposal, Lord. I know that you treasure the motive of my praise—not the means.

MAY 17

Let brotherly love continue. Be not forgetful to entertain strangers: for thereby some have entertained angels unawares.

—HEBREWS 13:1–2

THANK you for those people you have sent in my life who have been angels for me. Let me find ways to be an angel for others.

MAY 18

Blessed are the merciful: for they shall obtain mercy.

—MATTHEW 5:7

FOR those times when a friend or family member has forgiven me when I wronged them, I offer thanks and ask for your blessings upon them. They taught me about how powerful mercy can be. O merciful God, let me in turn be merciful to others.

MAY 19

Let thine heart keep my commandments: For length of days, and long life, and peace, shall they add to thee.

—PROVERBS 3:1–2

MAY you celebrate this day with all your heart.
Rejoice in the beauty of its light and warmth.
Give thanks for the air and grass and sidewalks.
Let gratitude for others flow into your soul.
And cherish the chance to work and play,
To think and speak—knowing this:
All simple pleasures are gifts to praise.

MAY 20

A soft answer turneth away wrath: but grievous words stir up anger.

—PROVERBS 15:1

DEAR God, isn't it funny how much better I feel when I choose to love? And yet how many times in the course of my life have I chosen anger or hatred or fear? Let me always choose love first, for when I do make that choice, it opens up the doorway to new friendships and joy that other choices cannot give me. Make love be not only my first choice but my only choice. Thank you, God, for choosing to love me.

MAY 21

“

O God, my heart is fixed; I will sing and give praise, even with my glory.

—PSALM 108:1

NOT everyone will praise you today, Lord, but I want to be one of those who does. I am grateful for your daily provision and presence. Let my voice be heard.

MAY 22

Many waters cannot quench love, neither can the floods drown it.

—SONG OF SOLOMON 8:7

GOD, I remember the day I met the love of my life. As our relationship developed, I could scarcely believe that there was even more to discover about one another. In fact, we were also alike in many intriguing ways. I am convinced that your love is reflected through our love. I am truly privileged to have such a special relationship. Thank you, God.

MAY 23

“

They that sow in tears shall reap in joy.

—PSALM 126:5

THE promise of hope fills the heart with a new perspective, and the eyes with a new vision. Darkness begins to lift, showing the path we could not see before, and a way out of our pain and suffering. The promise of hope opens doors we were certain were closed, and reveals solutions that evaded us. Hope is a key that unlocks the way to the blessings of God around us.

MAY 24

For God is not unrighteous to forget your work and labour of love, which ye have shewed toward his name.

—HEBREWS 6:10

I look around and see there is work to be done. Thank you for the gift of work to do. Guide my hands that they may help others. Guide my heart to see where there is need and how to respond to it. Guide my thoughts to know that even if I can only do a little, that is enough to make a difference.

MAY 25

Now there are diversities of gifts, but the same Spirit.

—1 CORINTHIANS 12:4

SO much to celebrate, Lord: waking to dawn gilding trees; squeezing fresh orange juice, its zest clinging to my hands all day; making a new friend, talking to an old one; watching the first leaf bud, raking the last. Each day's turning brings gifts from you to celebrate.

MAY 26

"

I will extol thee, my God, O king; and I will bless thy name for ever and ever.

—PSALM 145:1

YOU can only praise a king if he is a good king. And ours is. He is so good we will praise him for ever and ever. Take some time today to think about all the ways he is good to you and those you love.

MAY 27

“Come unto me, all ye that labour and are heavy laden, and I will give you rest.

—MATTHEW 11:28

O Lord, I know you take notice of them—the caretakers for the aged and the ill. They work selflessly for the most vulnerable among us, yet their efforts are so often overlooked. May they sense your presence beside them. May they feel your strength lifting them up and helping them through trying moments. Give them encouragement by helping them see what a difference they make in their patients' lives. Thank you for our helpers.

MAY 28

And the Lord God formed man of the dust of the ground, and breathed into his nostrils the breath of life; and man became a living soul.

—GENESIS 2:7

HOW easily, O God of eternity, for us to assume our time is like the grains of sand on an ocean beach—vast and endless. Remind us that each of our lives is limited like the sand in the hourglass. May what we do with that sand—play in it, work in it, build our relationships, whatever—be a wise use of this precious gift of living.

MAY 29

But these are written, that ye might believe that Jesus is the Christ, the Son of God; and that believing ye might have life through his name.

—JOHN 20:31

LORD, how many lives have been changed by the reforming, transforming power of your Word! So often I stumble upon a common verse, and it strikes me in a new, wonderful way. It brings breathtaking clarity when I need it most. Thank you for giving us your Word, Lord. We would be lost without it.

MAY 30

For we are his workmanship, created in Christ Jesus unto good works, which God hath before ordained that we should walk in them.

—EPHESIANS 2:10

LORD, what a miracle each newborn baby is. We marvel at the tiny hands and rosebud lips, and we know such a masterpiece could only come from you! We pray for all little children today, Lord. Watch over them and guide their parents. Grant all parents the courage, strength, and wisdom they need to fulfill their sacred duties.

MAY 31

“

It came even to pass, as the trumpeters and singers were as one, to make one sound to be heard in praising and thanking the Lord.

—2 CHRONICLES 5:13

PRAISE to our God is the basis of true unity, bringing God’s people together in joyful harmony. This isn’t just about the church choir. It is about the church and the gathering together of God’s people to praise him. Thank you, God, for providing us with this gathering place.

Daily Gratitude

JUNE

JUNE 1

Incline my heart unto thy testimonies, and not to covetousness. Turn away mine eyes from beholding vanity; and quicken thou me in thy way.

—PSALM 119:36–37

THE holiness of God is his complete and utter separation from our own weakness and self-centeredness. He is altogether lovely, over and above our limitations and failures. For this we rejoice, that a holy God is our helper and friend.

JUNE 2

The love of God is shed abroad in our hearts by the Holy Ghost which is given unto us.

—ROMANS 5:5

THOU who has given so much to me, give me one thing more: a grateful heart.

—George Herbert

JUNE 3

Hearken unto this, O Job: stand still, and consider the wondrous works of God. Dost thou know when God disposed them, and caused the light of his cloud to shine? Dost thou know the balancings of the clouds, the wondrous works of him which is perfect in knowledge?

—JOB 37:14–16

LORD, I can hear your voice in the bubbling brook, see your beauty in the petals of a flower, and feel your gentle breath in the evening breeze and in the soft kiss of a child. Thank you for all of these gifts.

JUNE 4

She openeth her mouth with wisdom; and in her tongue is the law of kindness.

—PROVERBS 31:26

THANK you, God, that I'm not the same person today as I was even just a few years ago. This new life as a parent writes its changing tale on my heart, face, and mind like growth rings on a tree. May this tree of life continue to grow into the future where I will provide limbs of love from which my children can launch their own lives.

JUNE 5

I thank my God upon every remembrance of you.

—PHILIPPIANS 1:3

PAUL was grateful for his friends at the church in Philippi. Every time he thought of them, he thanked God. Do you have friends like that? Take the time today to write them a note and let them know. So often we feel gratitude in our hearts but forget to share it with those we love.

JUNE 6

From the rising of the sun unto the going down of the same the Lord's name is to be praised.

—PSALM 113:3

LORD, you deserve my praise all day long—from the first cup of coffee in the morning until that final yawn at night. Your mercy and righteousness are consistent and constant. Please help my praise be the same.

JUNE 7

Whate'er my fears or foes suggest,
you are my hope, my joy, my rest.
My heart shall feel your love and raise
my cheerful voice to sing your praise.

—Isaac Watts

JUNE 8

By them shall the fowls of the heaven have their habitation, which sing among the branches. He watereth the hills from his chambers: the earth is satisfied with the fruit of thy works.

—PSALM 104:12–13

LISTEN to and appreciate the sparrow's song. It's soft and serene like a breeze whistling through the woods or a gurgling brook. It's an angelic song that resonates with heaven's voice.

JUNE 9

Happy is he that hath the God of Jacob for his help, whose hope is in the Lord his God: Which made heaven, and earth, the sea, and all that therein is: which keepeth truth for ever.

—PSALM 146:5–6

GOD, I feel happy today, and I have you to thank for that. No matter what is going on outside of me, I am strong and safe and secure inside because you love and care for me. Thank you for loving me when I have been cranky, tired, lazy, and even mean. Thank you for being there when I ignored your presence, God. Your steadfast love is a constant reminder of just how good I have it in life. And that makes me happiest of all!

JUNE 10

He that answereth a matter before he heareth it, it is folly and shame unto him.

—PROVERBS 18:13

TWO ears, one mouth? Perhaps a hint, subtle or not, about what is more important in life, great God. Make me at least as ready to listen as I am to talk. Give me patience to listen to the concerns, the hopes, the dreams of these important people called family, for that is how we connect. There are times to talk and times to listen. Please help me to know the difference.

JUNE 11

It is vain for you to rise up early, to sit up late, to eat the bread of sorrows: for so he giveth his beloved sleep.

—PSALM 127:2

O God of rest and rejuvenation, guide me to find ways to let your nurturing reach me. I need to be healthy and well-rested in order to provide, lead, and inspire. Burning the candle at both ends all the time is hardly an example I'm proud to set.

JUNE 12

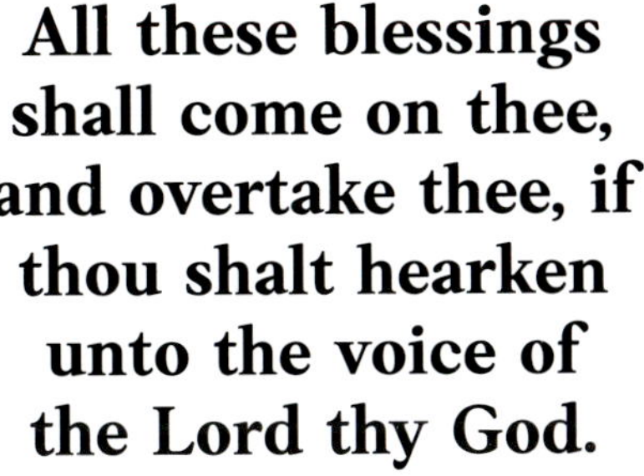

All these blessings shall come on thee, and overtake thee, if thou shalt hearken unto the voice of the Lord thy God.

—*DEUTERONOMY 28:2*

LORD, my heart overflows with gratitude for all the blessings you have sent into my life. I am cognizant of the fact that I am probably only aware of a small percentage of them though. You are such a generous God; you shower us with such abundance. I am grateful for it all, Lord.

JUNE 13

The angel came in unto her, and said, Hail, thou that art highly favoured, the Lord is with thee: blessed art thou among women.

—LUKE 1:28

THANK you, God, for such a wonderful role model as the mother of Jesus. So often we sanitize her life, forgetting she was a courageous, creative lady who loved with heart and hand and whose example I pledge to follow.

JUNE 14

As every man hath received the gift, even so minister the same one to another, as good stewards of the manifold grace of God.

—1 PETER 4:10

WHAT a blessing it is, God, to be able to earn a living for the family! To be free of worry about what they will eat, or what they will wear, or where they will sleep. You have given us so much: a house, flowers, a table and chairs, and even a camera to help us remember these days that are flying by so quickly. Yes, you have given. And your gifts are a serious calling: show us how to give in return!

JUNE 15

As ye know how we exhorted and comforted and charged every one of you, as a father doth his children, That ye would walk worthy of God, who hath called you unto his kingdom and glory.

—1 THESSALONIANS 2:11–12

HEAVENLY Father, today I am thankful for all the loving fathers and father figures. A dad conveys the dreams of his children to the ear of God.

JUNE 16

A man hath no better thing under the sun, than to eat, and to drink, and to be merry.

—ECCLESIASTES 8:15

LORD, some of our best family times occur when we can all sit down together to enjoy a meal and conversation. It's even better when we have company to share the fun.

After the blessing of food and family, everyone has a chance to be heard, humor is encouraged, and appetites flourish. Some of life's greatest problems are settled around our table.

Father, I am grateful that you are a God who wants us to enjoy ourselves. From my heart I thank you for the food that you supply, the closeness of our family, and the circle of love that surrounds us.

In this was manifested the love of God toward us, because that God sent his only begotten Son into the world, that we might live through him. Herein is love, not that we loved God, but that he loved us, and sent his Son to be the propitiation for our sins.

—1 JOHN 4:9–10

LIKE children with pail and shovel trying to empty the ocean into a hole dug in the sand, O God, we can't begin to fathom the enormity of the love with which you long to fill us.

JUNE 18

Give thanks unto the Lord, call upon his name, make known his deeds among the people.

—1 CHRONICLES 16:8

TELL someone today what God has done for you or for someone you love. Praise God for the many miracles around you. Songs, testimonies, and prayers are all ways to do this. And it needs to be done.

JUNE 19

Know ye not that ye are the temple of God, and that the Spirit of God dwelleth in you? If any man defile the temple of God, him shall God destroy; for the temple of God is holy, which temple ye are.

—1 CORINTHIANS 3:16–17

HOW marvelous our bodies! May we care for them today with all the reverence and honor we might extend toward any great gift that defies explanation.

JUNE 20

Humble yourselves therefore under the mighty hand of God, that he may exalt you in due time: Casting all your care upon him; for he careth for you.

—1 PETER 5:6–7

ALMIGHTY God, why is it we don't remember that you alone are the source of all comfort? Instead, when times are tough, we seek comfort in the things of the world we see around us—in too much food, drink, or late-night television. Those things can distract us, but we know they can never comfort us the way you do. Thank you for your faithfulness, Lord. For at the end of every one of our fruitless searches you are there, and in your presence we find true comfort.

JUNE 21

Now learn a parable of the fig tree; When her branch is yet tender, and putteth forth leaves, ye know that summer is near.

—MARK 13:28

THANK you for the bright colors of summer! I look around and see the sun in the sky, the clear moon in the night, the brilliance of the flowers and the trees. Thank you, Lord, for blessing me with color in my life. I know that even the darkest, dreariest days cannot last forever, just as the memory of winter fades during summer's glory.

JUNE 22

Thanks be unto God for his unspeakable gift.

—2 CORINTHIANS 9:15

SOME gifts are so great we can't describe the gift or our response to it. The gospel is such a gift, beyond our comprehension or expectation, bringing both peace with God and from God through Jesus Christ. Thank the Lord today for this unspeakable gift.

JUNE 23

I have called upon thee, for thou wilt hear me, O God: incline thine ear unto me, and hear my speech.

—PSALM 17:6

HOW good it is to talk to God! Formal prayer is important, but today I just want to pour out my heart and speak to God in my own words. Thank you for the opportunity to talk to you as a friend. Thank you for listening to my prayers and understanding my heart.

JUNE 24

Therefore, brethren, stand fast, and hold the traditions which ye have been taught, whether by word, or our epistle.

—2 THESSALONIANS 2:15

I do not take enough time to appreciate my heritage. Thank you, God, for giving me this gift. Let me take time to recall special traditions from my homeland and remember to pass them on to my children. I am grateful for the heritage that makes me special yet links me to countless other people in the past, present, and future.

JUNE 25

It is a good thing to give thanks unto the Lord, and to sing praises unto thy name, O Most High.

—PSALM 92:1

OUR God is most high. There is none higher or more worthy of praise. So, it is a good thing to give thanks to the Lord. He is over and beyond all your troubles. Lean on him in difficult times and express your gratitude for his abundant love.

JUNE 26

For the Lord thy God bringeth thee into a good land, a land of brooks of water, of fountains and depths that spring out of valleys and hills; A land of wheat, and barley, and vines, and fig trees, and pomegranates; a land of oil olive, and honey; A land wherein thou shalt eat bread without scarceness, thou shalt not lack any thing in it.

—DEUTERONOMY 8:7–9

EVER notice how the more grateful you are for the good things in your life, the more the floodgates tend to open, bringing even more gifts? We lack for nothing when we are grateful for everything. That is when the blessings become a stream that never ceases to provide us with more to appreciate.

JUNE 27

They cried unto the Lord in their trouble, and he delivered them out of their distresses.

—PSALM 107:6

SOMEWHERE on this road of life you will need to be rescued, whether you realize it or not. Every night be grateful—just in case today was that day.

JUNE 28

Pride goeth before destruction, and an haughty spirit before a fall. Better it is to be of an humble spirit with the lowly, than to divide the spoil with the proud.

—PROVERBS 16:18–19

MOST of us realize that we are naturally self-centered, and we often respond to those around us in ways that make us appear proud, haughty, or arrogant. But if we look at Jesus' life, we see an excellent example of humility—an example that we should strive to follow. He taught that pride is destructive, but humility is powerful. Rather than touting his own greatness, Jesus was willing to kneel down and wash the feet of others, to show that we should all be servants to each other—and to God.

JUNE 29

But the mercy of the Lord is from everlasting to everlasting upon them that fear him, and his righteousness unto children's children; To such as keep his covenant, and to those that remember his commandments to do them.

—PSALM 103:17–18

BLESS my family, O God, for it is unique. I am grateful you know we are joined by love—for each other and for you. We are grateful you use more than one pattern to create a good family. This pioneering family has you at its heart.

JUNE 30

I do set my bow in the cloud, and it shall be for a token of a covenant between me and the earth.

—GENESIS 9:13

THANK you, Lord, for the beauty of a rainbow. What a contrast that peaceful, glowing bow is to the tempest of the storm that came before it! Help me see rainbows as your promise to the world that beauty and happiness can come after pain and brighten my world again.

Daily Gratitude

JULY

JULY 1

Little drops of water,
Little grains of sand,
Make the mighty ocean
And the pleasant land.
Little deeds of kindness,
Little words of love,
Help to make earth happy
Like the heaven above.

—Julia Fletcher Carney

JULY 2

Let every one of us please his neighbour for his good to edification.

—ROMANS 15:2

A good neighbor is a blessing! I am so grateful for the neighbors I have known and who have become my friends just by virtue of living close by. Together we have faced problems and shared memories. Thank you, Lord, for giving me good neighbors who will stand beside me and help make all our lives more complete.

JULY 3

Make a joyful noise unto God, all ye lands.

—PSALM 66:1

THANK you for fireworks! They're a summer sight that I love to see, full of exuberance and creativity. Thank you for the times we have cause to celebrate and gather together to admire and share in this beauty.

JULY 4

For, brethren, ye have been called unto liberty; only use not liberty for an occasion to the flesh, but by love serve one another.

—*GALATIANS 5:13*

HOW blessed I am to live in the United States! Life may not always be easy, but I am grateful for the freedoms this nation gives to me. Thank you, Lord, for all the people who fought to make this country a free and beautiful land. I remember those patriots today as I listen to fireworks and enjoy my freedom. May I never take that freedom for granted.

JULY 5

I will praise thee, O Lord, among the people: I will sing unto thee among the nations.

—PSALM 57:9

LORD, help me sing your praises. I don't need an actual song, guitar, or piano. I just need a grateful heart and a worthy subject. Please Lord, be the subject of my song today.

JULY 6

Therefore we are always confident, knowing that, whilst we are at home in the body, we are absent from the Lord: (For we walk by faith, not by sight:) We are confident, I say, and willing rather to be absent from the body, and to be present with the Lord.

—2 CORINTHIANS 5:6–8

FAITH is the root of all blessings. Believe and you shall be saved; believe and you will be satisfied; believe, and you cannot but be comforted and happy.

—Jeremy Taylor

JULY 7

Train up a child in the way he should go: and when he is old, he will not depart from it.

—PROVERBS 22:6

ONE of my kids talked back to me today, God—and you gave me the grace to handle it well! I know this is something I struggle with, teaching and allowing independence while also instilling values of respect. I've brought this to you in prayer so many times. And today it felt like that habit of prayer paid off; I took a breath and was able to be loving in my response. Thank you, Lord.

JULY 8

Continue in prayer, and watch in the same with thanksgiving.

—COLOSSIANS 4:2

MAY your day be filled with prayer, as you bring every need and concern before the throne of God. But do it with thanksgiving, for the God who hears your prayer will answer it.

JULY 9

Let us not therefore judge one another any more: but judge this rather, that no man put a stumbling block or an occasion to fall in his brother's way. I know, and am persuaded by the Lord Jesus, that there is nothing unclean of itself: but to him that esteemeth any thing to be unclean, to him it is unclean.

—ROMANS 14:13–14

GOD, thank you for the people that inspire me to accept others. Let me learn to love everyone—including myself. Amen.

JULY 10

And there shall be a tabernacle for a shadow in the day time from the heat, and for a place of refuge, and for a covert from storm and from rain.

—ISAIAH 4:6

BLESS this roof over our heads, and keep it from leaking. But more than that, move us to give thanks for the next rainstorm. Because you are more than a good roof—we need to remember that. And our neighbors' gardens need watering more than we need to stay dry.

JULY 11

For as the body without the spirit is dead, so faith without works is dead also.

—JAMES 2:26

JUST as our bodies absorb the warmth of the sun, our souls absorb the warmth of God's love.

JULY 12

"

Now our Lord Jesus Christ himself, and God, even our Father, which hath loved us, and hath given us everlasting consolation and good hope through grace, comfort your hearts, and stablish you in every good word and work.

—2 THESSALONIANS 2:16–17

LORD, as I walk in your spirit of strength and love today, may others see what life in you is like. It isn't mere religion or a list of rules and regulations. Rather it's real life full of adventure, challenge, wonder, joy, and peace—all in the context of my relationship with you as I live through the energy you provide. Thank you, Lord, for the spirit of boldness that enables me to live out my faith without fear.

JULY 13

But we see Jesus, who was made a little lower than the angels for the suffering of death, crowned with glory and honour; that he by the grace of God should taste death for every man.

—HEBREWS 2:9

JESUS, how can we express our gratitude, that you died to save us all? How else but by saying to the Father, as you did in the Garden, "nevertheless not what I will, but what thou wilt." (Mark 14:36)

JULY 14

He hath made every thing beautiful in his time: also he hath set the world in their heart, so that no man can find out the work that God maketh from the beginning to the end.

—ECCLESIASTES 3:11

WE live in an age of technological wonders! How amazing it is to be able to connect with old friends and distant cousins from hundreds of miles away. Let me use technology to make my circle of love wider, to bring your love to more people. Let me be warm and inviting in a way that conveys your love and points people towards you.

JULY 15

“Hear my prayer, O Lord, and give ear unto my cry; hold not thy peace at my tears.

—PSALM 39:12

SOMETIMES my heart is so overwhelmed, God, that I don’t know where to begin my prayer. Help me to quiet my soul and remember that you know everything inside of my mind before I ever come to you with it. Still, I need to tell you about it, Lord, and I know you want me to tell you. Thank you for being such a faithful listener and for caring about everything that concerns me. When I remember that, it helps me slow down, take a deep breath, and begin the conversation.

JULY 16

Shew me thy ways, O Lord; teach me thy paths.

—PSALM 25:4

HOW grateful we are, God of knowledge, that you created us so curious. In your wisdom, it is the searcher turning over every leaf who finds four-leaf clovers; the doubter who invents; and the determined, like a duckling pecking its way from the shell, who emerges strong enough to fly.

JULY 17

I will both lay me down in peace, and sleep: for thou, Lord, only makest me dwell in safety.

—PSALM 4:8

WHAT a wonderful day! And now, God of rest and peace, the children are sleeping, replete with the joys of our summer discoveries that they are savoring to the last drop. We celebrate the joy of ordinary days and rest in your care.

JULY 18

Let your conversation be without covetousness; and be content with such things as ye have: for he hath said, I will never leave thee, nor forsake thee.

—HEBREWS 13:5

FATHER God, you are the giver of all gifts. All of our resources and all we have came from you, and they are only ours for a little while. Protect us from any addiction to material things. Gently remind us when we have enough—enough to eat, enough to wear, enough to enjoy. Most of all, keep us mindful of the fact that because we have you, we have everything we need.

JULY 19

While we look not at the things which are seen, but at the things which are not seen: for the things which are seen are temporal; but the things which are not seen are eternal.

—2 CORINTHIANS 4:18

LORD, I never imagined when I was young that growing older could be such a blessing. The experience and the wisdom I have now about how life works—these are gifts I would never trade for anything. Some people dread their later years, but mine are so blessed—I can only imagine how good the rest of my days will be. Thank you, Lord, for allowing me the privilege of getting older.

JULY 20

Beloved, if God so loved us, we ought also to love one another. No man hath seen God at any time. If we love one another, God dwelleth in us, and his love is perfected in us.

—1 JOHN 4:11–12

COUNT on your family, especially when it comes time to count your blessings.

JULY 21

Let every thing that hath breath praise the Lord. Praise ye the Lord.

—PSALM 150:6

YOUR cat, purring gently on your lap, or your dog, wagging his tail in joy—these too are reasons to be grateful to God who created all creatures great or small. The Lord God made them all.

JULY 22

I prayed for an angel to comfort me
at night.

I prayed for an angel to make the
darkness bright.

When the long night was over and
the pain was all gone,

I thanked God for the angel who kept
me safe until dawn.

JULY 23

By faith Noah, being warned of God of things not seen as yet, moved with fear, prepared an ark to the saving of his house; by the which he condemned the world, and became heir of the righteousness which is by faith.

—HEBREWS 11:7

THANK you, Lord, for the fact that when difficulties and trouble start to accumulate like waters at flood stage, I can find the high ground of safety and security in you. I trust you today—trust your goodness as well as your promises of protection and care for me. And even if everything I own is swept away in the flood, you will still be there with me. Remind me that the stuff of this world is temporary, but my life in you is kept safe both now and for eternity.

JULY 24

I will love thee, O Lord, my strength. The Lord is my rock, and my fortress, and my deliverer; my God, my strength, in whom I will trust; my buckler, and the horn of my salvation, and my high tower.

—PSALM 18:1–2

AFTER you recover from a crisis, you are better able to help others. God strengthened you; now he can use you to strengthen others. Thank God for granting you resilience.

JULY 25

Then were there brought unto him little children, that he should put his hands on them, and pray: and the disciples rebuked them. But Jesus said, Suffer little children, and forbid them not, to come unto me: for of such is the kingdom of heaven.

—MATTHEW 19:13–14

LORD, today I want to give you thanks for all the little children who bring so much joy into the world. I feel that they must spring directly from your love for us. How we treasure the hugs and smiles of these little angels, Lord. They are as special to us as they are to you. Lay your hand upon their heads, Lord. Touch them with your grace, and keep them close to you.

JULY 26

He fill thy mouth with laughing, and thy lips with rejoicing.

—JOB 8:21

TODAY I am thankful for the gift of laughter. How wonderful it is to let out a big belly laugh and feel joy rush through my entire body! Thank you for the people who make me laugh, whether it is a neighbor, friend, or performer on television. Thank you for allowing me to experience joy bursting out of me, and help me make others feel happy with my laughter as well.

JULY 27

The Lord hath done great things for us; whereof we are glad.

—PSALM 126:3

LORD, how good have you been to me? Let me count the ways! In times of discouragement all I need to do is sit quietly and remember all the times in the past when you stepped in to set wrongs right, gave me a second chance, or showed up with a last-minute miracle. Lord, you are so good. May my faith never waver in view of all the wonders you have wrought!

JULY 28

And blessed be his glorious name for ever: and let the whole earth be filled with his glory; Amen, and Amen.

—PSALM 72:19

WE sit around the table, my family and I, and celebrate the blessings God has given us. Blessings of loved ones, of good food, and of the shared bounty of the earth. Blessings of a warm, happy home filled with laughter and joy. Blessings of times spent together, of achievements and successes. Blessings of lessons we've learned, of silver linings surrounding every dark cloud, and of rainbows following every dreary shower. But mostly we celebrate our faith; in ourselves, in each other, and in God. Faith is the foundation of our strength, the bedrock of our joy.

JULY 29

And what is the exceeding greatness of his power to us-ward who believe, according to the working of his mighty power, Which he wrought in Christ, when he raised him from the dead, and set him at his own right hand in the heavenly places.

—EPHESIANS 1:19–20

THANK you, Lord, for the signs of your power. Thank you for the awe I feel during a thunderstorm or at the sight of a monument in nature. Thank you for the thrill I feel when I see one of your works in all its glory. It is good to know your power and feel its presence in my life.

JULY 30

Therefore I say unto you, Take no thought for your life, what ye shall eat, or what ye shall drink; nor yet for your body, what ye shall put on. Is not the life more than meat, and the body than raiment?

—*MATTHEW 6:25*

LORD, sometimes I worry about my loved ones. Though I often complain of the monotony of my day-to-day life, I know my days are full of moments to be treasured. When I hear shocking, horrific stories on the news, I often wonder how I would handle such events if they were to befall me or a loved one. Father, I cling to your promise that you give each of us a future filled with hope. I am grateful that you hear me when I come to you in prayer. Please stay close to me and my loved ones. Grant us the strength to prevail in all circumstances.

JULY 31

Fear thou not; for I am with thee: be not dismayed; for I am thy God: I will strengthen thee; yea, I will help thee; yea, I will uphold thee with the right hand of my righteousness.

—ISAIAH 41:10

I am still moving, God, through storms. By your grace—over rough country, you have carried me; amidst pounding waves, you have held me; beyond the horizon of my longings, you have shown me your purposes. Even in this small room, sitting still, I am moving closer to you, God.

Daily Gratitude
AUGUST

AUGUST 1

“

Oh that men would praise the Lord for his goodness, and for his wonderful works to the children of men!

—PSALM 107:21

THE most important prayer in the world is just two words long: “Thank You.”
—Meister Eckhart

AUGUST 2

And he hath put a new song in my mouth, even praise unto our God: many shall see it, and fear, and shall trust in the Lord.

—PSALM 40:3

PLEASE, Father, widen my influence today. May many see and hear how grateful I am for your love and grace. And may they trust you as I trust you, with reverence and awe.

AUGUST 3

"

Now the God of hope fill you with all joy and peace in believing, that ye may abound in hope, through the power of the Holy Ghost.

—*ROMANS 15:13*

THERE are many aspects of life that are easy to take for granted: the air that I breathe, the rain for the crops, the food that I eat, and the relationships that I have. I sometimes forget how blessed I am. I want to take time every day to really contemplate how faithfully you work in my life. Once all of your blessings are fresh in my mind, it will be impossible to hide my gratitude. Your faithfulness will be on the tip of my tongue and in the innermost recesses of my heart.

AUGUST 4

From the end of the earth will I cry unto thee, when my heart is overwhelmed: lead me to the rock that is higher than I.

—*PSALM 61:2*

INSTEAD of feeling overwrought with demands to the point of being overwhelmed, feel the overflowing joy that comes from daily life in the midst of a hustling, bustling family. The two halves make one marvelous whole of God's balance. Thank God for family.

AUGUST 5

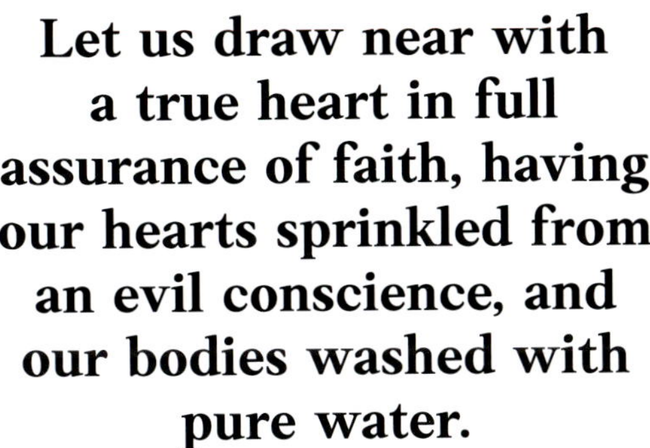

Let us draw near with a true heart in full assurance of faith, having our hearts sprinkled from an evil conscience, and our bodies washed with pure water.

—HEBREWS 10:22

I remember it—coming from a swim and lying back in white sand—the gift of a moment to rest, to sit in reverie, to watch, to close eyes and think of nothing but the sound of breaking waves. Yes, you were there with the sounds and the sunshine, and I am thankful.

AUGUST 6

"

The Lord thy God in the midst of thee is mighty; he will save, he will rejoice over thee with joy; he will rest in his love, he will joy over thee with singing.

—ZEPHANIAH 3:17

GOD, when I am tired and just feeling down about everything in my life, your love reminds me that there is a spring of hope and renewal I can drink from anytime. It may take me awhile to come around, but I always come back to love as the reason to keep on going, even when my gas tank is empty. Love fuels me and gets me back out on the road of life, ready for whatever new challenge you have in store for me.

AUGUST 7

In all things, give thanks.

In the good days of laughter and joy,
give thanks.

In the bad days of struggle and strife,
give thanks.

In the face of fortune and misfortune,
give thanks.

In the presence of pleasure and pain,
give thanks.

In all things, give thanks.

For lessons and blessings are found
not just in light but in darkness.

AUGUST 8

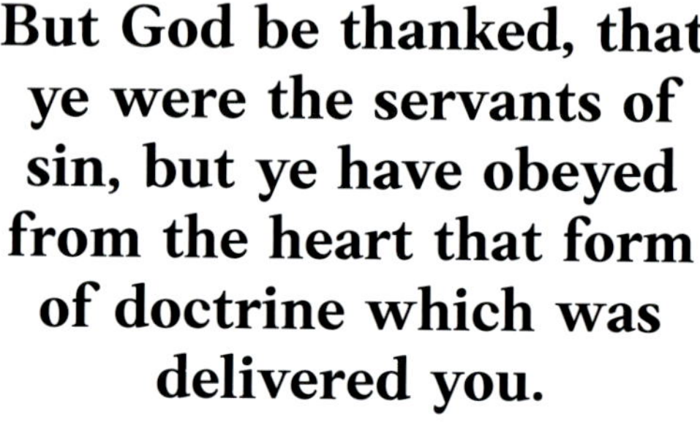

But God be thanked, that ye were the servants of sin, but ye have obeyed from the heart that form of doctrine which was delivered you.

—*ROMANS 6:17*

BY God's grace, we are no longer the servants of sin. This is remarkable and worthy of our gratitude. With God's help, we can now obey him from the heart. May God be praised.

AUGUST 9

"

Let my mouth be filled with thy praise and with thy honour all the day.

—PSALM 71:8

CAN you honor God all day? When you awake in the morning, can you praise him? Can you sing along to worship music on your way to and from work? Cultivate an attitude of gratitude, and let your mouth be filled with praise.

AUGUST 10

He shall feed his flock like a shepherd: he shall gather the lambs with his arm, and carry them in his bosom, and shall gently lead those that are with young.

—ISAIAH 40:11

FATHER in heaven, when all else fails, I turn to you for the comfort only you can provide. I have done all I can do, and now I rest in the belief that you are taking from me my burdens and doing for me what I cannot. In you alone do I find that comforting assurance that everything is being taken care of and that all will work out as it should. My surrender to your comfort is not out of weakness but out of my faith in your eternal love and concern for me. For that I am grateful.

AUGUST 11

“

For where two or three are gathered together in my name, there am I in the midst of them.

—MATTHEW 18:20

LORD, if only everyone could adopt your law of love as our neighbors have. I am grateful for their kindness, their willingness, and their generous spirits. Bless these loving people, Father, who are your hands reaching out to care for us. Please make me a good neighbor to them, and may I find many opportunities to return your love by helping them when they are in need.

AUGUST 12

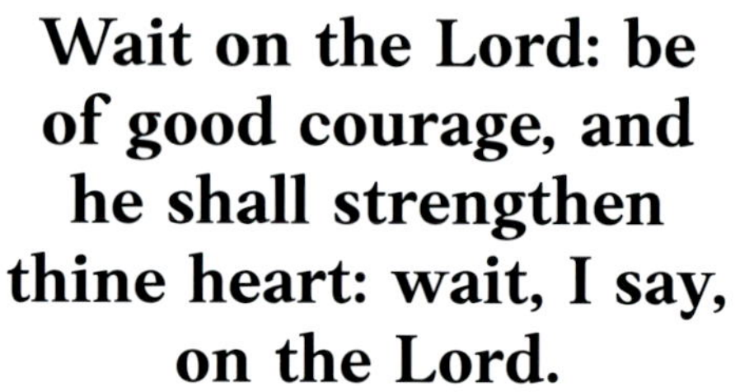

Wait on the Lord: be of good courage, and he shall strengthen thine heart: wait, I say, on the Lord.

—PSALM 27:14

IN this day of bigger is best, Lord, we wonder what difference our little lights can make. Remind us of the laser, so tiny, yet when focused, has infinite power. This little light of mine, O Lord, give it such focus.

AUGUST 13

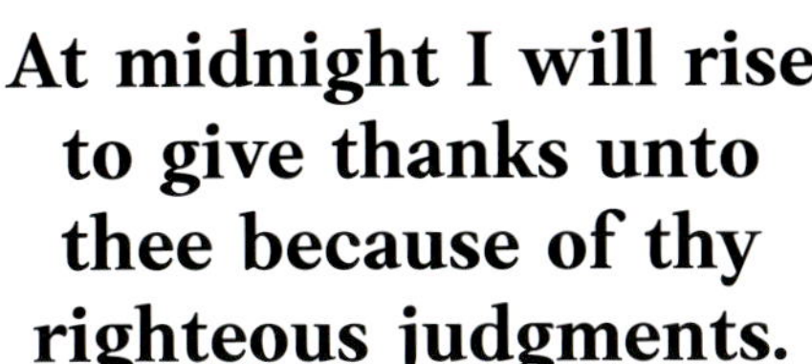

At midnight I will rise to give thanks unto thee because of thy righteous judgments.

—*PSALM 119:62*

DO you wake up in the middle of the night? Instead of lying there fitfully, start to thank God that he always does the right thing. Mediate on this truth and be at peace. Allow the loving presence of our Father to calm you.

AUGUST 14

The flowers appear on the earth; the time of the singing of birds is come, and the voice of the turtle is heard in our land.

—SONG OF SOLOMON 2:12

TAKING an evening walk around my neighborhood, I pass both beautifully cultivated gardens with colorful roses and the edges of a forest preserve, where small, bright wildflowers peep from the brush. I thank you for the beauty that both of them bring into the world. Your creations are wonderful, Lord!

AUGUST 15

"

Trust in the Lord with all thine heart; and lean not unto thine own understanding. In all thy ways acknowledge him, and he shall direct thy paths.

—PROVERBS 3:5–6

THE past, O God of yesterdays, todays, and promise-filled tomorrows, can be an anchor or a launching pad. It's sometimes so easy to look back on the pain and hurt and believe the future may be an instant replay. Help us to accept the aches of the past and put them in perspective so we can also see the many ways you supported and nurtured us. Then, believing in your promise of regeneration, launch us into the future free and excited to live in joy.

AUGUST 16

"

Jesus called a little child unto him, and set him in the midst of them, And said, Verily I say unto you, Except ye be converted, and become as little children, ye shall not enter into the kingdom of heaven.

—*MATTHEW 18:2–3*

THANK you, Lord, for the gift of play returned to me in the hands of grandchildren. Keep me agile and ready to drop whatever task is tethering me to routine and follow where I am led, even across a goal line scuffed in the driveway dust.

AUGUST 17

And the Lord answered me, and said, Write the vision, and make it plain upon tables, that he may run that readeth it.

—HABAKKUK 2:2

SOME people have the ability to write words that lift the heart and soothe the soul. Let's thank God for those who serve us in this way.

AUGUST 18

"

I know both how to be abased, and I know how to abound: every where and in all things I am instructed both to be full and to be hungry, both to abound and to suffer need. I can do all things through Christ which strengtheneth me.

—PHILIPPIANS 4:12–13

AN attitude of gratitude can help you get through even the roughest of times. Focusing on God's blessings helps you realize just how loved you are. It isn't about ignoring all the things that go wrong or bring you suffering but always remembering to look for the blessing in the lesson and the silver lining in the dark clouds above.

AUGUST 19

And ye now therefore have sorrow: but I will see you again, and your heart shall rejoice, and your joy no man taketh from you.

—JOHN 16:22

O Lord Almighty, what comfort I find in your constancy and faithfulness. You are the same God who hung the stars in the universe and called them by name. You've heard the prayers of troubled souls since the beginning of time, and yet you never stop listening. Thank you, Lord, for your constant sovereignty and your unfailing love. You are indeed our comfort and our strength when all about us seems to be falling apart.

AUGUST 20

"

Rejoice with them that do rejoice, and weep with them that weep. Be of the same mind one toward another.

—ROMANS 12:15–16

IN my attempts to "get it right" as I order my life and the lives of those in my family, remind me, God, to look around and see how you have brought order to our world. Such balance, such harmony, such stability. May I find the faith to trust you like a bird trusts the winds that allow it to soar.

AUGUST 21

“

Praise ye the Lord: for it is good to sing praises unto our God; for it is pleasant; and praise is comely.

—PSALM 147:1

GRATITUDE is not a duty; it is a pleasure. Such an attitude is attractive, transforming our bitterness and fatigue into songs of joy. Bring forward this good attitude to inspire yourself and those around you, feeling the glory of God in each expression of gratitude.

AUGUST 22

"

The Lord is my light and my salvation; whom shall I fear? The Lord is the strength of my life; of whom shall I be afraid?

—PSALM 27:1

LORD, you are the light I follow down this long, dark tunnel. You are the voice that whispers, urging me onward when this wall of sorrow seems insurmountable. You are the hand that reaches out and grabs mine when I feel as if I'm sinking in despair. You alone, Lord, are the waters that fill me when I am dried of all hope and faith. I thank you, Lord, for although I may feel like giving up, you have not given up on me.

AUGUST 23

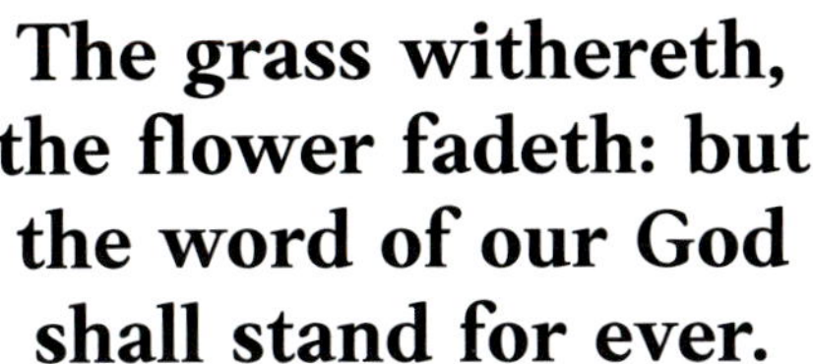

The grass withereth, the flower fadeth: but the word of our God shall stand for ever.

—ISAIAH 40:8

LORD, I've stood by too many deathbeds to ever doubt that the adage "you can't take it with you" is absolutely true. We come into this world with nothing, and we leave with nothing. So why is it so tempting to spend so much of our time striving for more money and possessions? We forget all those things are fleeting and the only people who are impressed by what we accumulate are those whose values are worldly. But you, O God, are eternal! Thank you for providing a way for us to be with you forever.

AUGUST 24

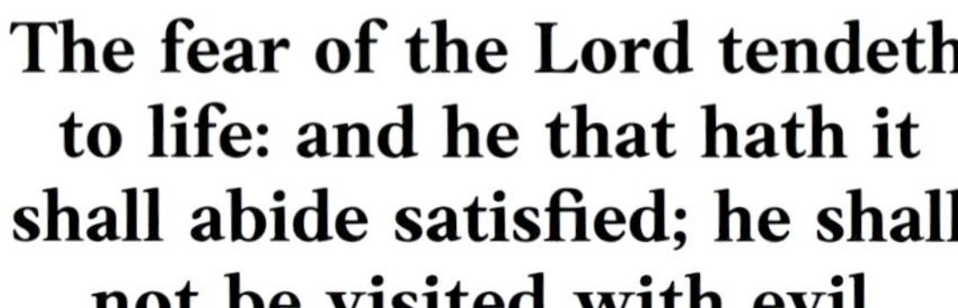

The fear of the Lord tendeth to life: and he that hath it shall abide satisfied; he shall not be visited with evil.

—PROVERBS 19:23

CHERISH the chance to work and play and think and speak and sing; all simple pleasures are opportunities for grateful praise.

AUGUST 25

“

Commit thy works unto the Lord, and thy thoughts shall be established.

—PROVERBS 16:3

WORK is good right now, God of all labor, and I think I know why: You and I are working together. Is this what it is to be called? I think it must be, for you are the source of my talents, for which I am grateful. Through the support of others, gifted teachers, mentors, and leaders, and through those willing to take a chance on me despite the odds, you have always been present, and I am grateful for that.

AUGUST 26

“

Speaking to yourselves in psalms and hymns and spiritual songs, singing and making melody in your heart to the Lord.

—EPHESIANS 5:19

MUSIC fills my heart today! I am so grateful for music in all its forms: the loud thump of rock music, the pretty complexities of a classical symphony, the simple melody of a whistled tune. Thank you, God, for putting music into the world and letting it fill my heart with emotion.

AUGUST 27

"

Honour all men. Love the brotherhood. Fear God. Honour the king.

—1 PETER 2:17

LET us revive the custom of blessing. When we bless someone, we show love and respect, encouraging greatness and pride. Sincerely honoring the people in our lives is a wonderful way of showing gratitude to the Lord.

AUGUST 28

"

Hatred stirreth up strifes: but love covereth all sins.

—PROVERBS 10:12

THANK you for the difficult people in my life. They show me that not everything can be easy. When I try to connect with someone who is hard to get along with or who doesn't agree with me, I think of how Jesus reached out even to those who did not agree with him. Allow me to be like Jesus and be thankful for the opportunity to extend my heart to everyone.

AUGUST 29

“

The Spirit itself beareth witness with our spirit, that we are the children of God.

—ROMANS 8:16

THE noise of my children fills my heart. I rejoice in their laughter and loud voices. Some days I may not appreciate the tumult children bring into my life. Help me to appreciate their moods, even when they are not always bright and happy. Lead me to be grateful for how much fun childhood can be. Thank you for letting me join my children in enjoying this special time.

AUGUST 30

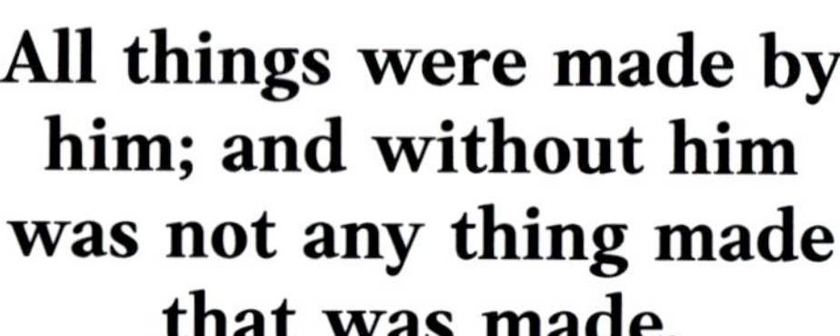

All things were made by him; and without him was not any thing made that was made.

—JOHN 1:3

IT is easy to praise you for your majesty and power when we see thundering waterfalls, crashing ocean waves, or majestic sunsets. Help us learn to praise you when we see a dewdrop, a seedling, or an ant.

AUGUST 31

"

As for me and my house, we will serve the Lord.

—JOSHUA 24:15

THE love and devotion of family serve as the foundation upon which dreams are built. The trustworthiness of family creates a sanctuary that can be depended upon in times of struggle. The blessings of family bolster the spirit. The pride of family enthuses the heart. With a loving family standing behind you, it becomes much easier to stand on your own. Thank you, God, for my family.

Daily Gratitude

SEPTEMBER

SEPTEMBER 1

Of all good gifts that the Lord lets fall,
Is not silence the best of all?

The deep, sweet hush when the song is closed,
And every sound but a voiceless ghost;

And every sigh, as we listening leant,
A breathless quiet of vast content?

The laughs we laughed have a purer ring
With but their memory echoing;

So of all good gifts that the Lord lets fall,
Is not silence the best of all?

—James Whitcomb Riley

SEPTEMBER 2

And whatsoever ye do in word or deed, do all in the name of the Lord Jesus, giving thanks to God and the Father by him.

—COLOSSIANS 3:17

FATHER, today I want to speak and act in your name and for your glory. I need your help though. Please, Father, give me your wisdom and give me your strength, and I will give you praise.

SEPTEMBER 3

"Drop down, ye heavens, from above, and let the skies pour down righteousness: let the earth open, and let them bring forth salvation, and let righteousness spring up together; I the Lord have created it.

—ISAIAH 45:8

RAIN patters down, making puddles everywhere. I wasn't expecting the rain, but I am grateful for its beauty. I look up and see the thickness of the gray clouds and think of a soft blanket. I listen to the rain pour down and think of how it waters the earth to bring new life. Thank you, Lord, for the gift of a rainy day.

SEPTEMBER 4

Hear counsel, and receive instruction, that thou mayest be wise in thy latter end.

—PROVERBS 19:20

THANK you, God, for the wisdom to know when to speak, what to say, and how to say it. Guard my mouth today from any form of foolishness, that in all circumstances I might honor you with my words.

SEPTEMBER 5

Draw nigh to God, and he will draw nigh to you.

—JAMES 4:8

GOD, it's that time again, when my children are off to school, when my house becomes a little less noisy, and when my life becomes a little less hectic. I will miss them, but I will also cherish this time for me. Time to work on my own life, time to follow my own dreams, time to listen to the prompting of my own inner voice. As the days grow shorter outside, let me make use of my time in the highest and best ways. Let me be me for a while, until they come back home again.

SEPTEMBER 6

"

Truly the light is sweet, and a pleasant thing it is for the eyes to behold the sun.

—*ECCLESIASTES 11:7*

BE thankful for all of creation. Embrace the hope of each new morning and the last ray of sunshine that falls at day's end.

SEPTEMBER 7

“

All scripture is given by inspiration of God, and is profitable for doctrine, for reproof, for correction, for instruction in righteousness: That the man of God may be perfect, thoroughly furnished unto all good works.

—2 TIMOTHY 3:16–17

LORD, how grateful I am for the wise leaders who came before me. Reading old journals, books, and accounts of their lives, I see how you were as active in their lives as you are in ours today. Reading about the past gives us hope and inspiration for the future, and we come away reassured that you are always with us. Thank you, Lord, for your steadfast love through all generations.

SEPTEMBER 8

"

A sound heart is the life of the flesh: but envy the rottenness of the bones.

—PROVERBS 14:30

LORD God, why is it that we tend to hold so tightly to the things of this world? We know in our hearts that everything we have is ours only by your grace and great generosity. When we accumulate more than we need, it only builds barriers between ourselves and you. Thank you for your provision, Lord. May we learn to hold everything loosely, knowing it is only borrowed.

"

Mine hand also hath laid the foundation of the earth, and my right hand hath spanned the heavens: when I call unto them, they stand up together.

—ISAIAH 48:13

HEAVENLY Father, when you made the earth, you were satisfied with the job and pronounced it "good." Because I am your child, I find satisfaction in creating too. I give you thanks, Father, for the gift of creativity. Only you can satisfy our longing souls by filling them with creative achievement.

SEPTEMBER 10

"

But the wisdom that is from above is first pure, then peaceable, gentle, and easy to be intreated, full of mercy and good fruits, without partiality, and without hypocrisy.

—JAMES 3:17

WHEN I read this verse, I realize how perfectly Jesus personified heavenly wisdom. It's a wonder to me that we are called to walk in his footsteps, but then I remember that it is only possible to do it through the Spirit that works in and through us. Thank you, Lord, for making the things of heaven available to those who seek them.

SEPTEMBER 11

"

We are troubled on every side, yet not distressed; we are perplexed, but not in despair; Persecuted, but not forsaken; cast down, but not destroyed.

—2 CORINTHIANS 4:8–9

THIS is a sad and solemn day, yet there is still time to be thankful. Thank you, Lord, for all the emergency workers who help people every day. They bring light to the darkness and help to those who need it most. Thank you for their selflessness and willingness to give everything they have to save another. Just as Jesus sacrificed his life to save us, we are blessed by the sacrifices of those who save our lives.

SEPTEMBER 12

"

Bless the Lord, ye his angels, that excel in strength, that do his commandments, hearkening unto the voice of his word.

—PSALM 103:20

FATHER, the wind rustling the leaves reminds me of angel wings all around me. Thank you for such a reminder. Help me stay mindful that the work of angels goes on all the time all around me whether I am aware or not, and that life is even more than I see.

SEPTEMBER 13

"

Jesus saith unto them, Yea; have ye never read, Out of the mouth of babes and sucklings thou hast perfected praise?

—MATTHEW 21:16

O Lord, what a blessing children are in this world. They bring such joy into our lives and are a precious composite of the best of our past and the hopes for the future. Thank you for your love for all children, Lord. Please guard them always.

SEPTEMBER 14

"

Rejoice in the Lord, ye righteous; and give thanks at the remembrance of his holiness.

—PSALM 97:12

BE grateful for God's Word today. Be grateful for his promises. Be grateful for the stories of imperfect but faithful men and women. Be grateful for the gospel itself. In all things be grateful and fear not.

SEPTEMBER 15

A friend loveth at all times, and a brother is born for adversity.

—PROVERBS 17:17

DURING challenging times, I thank you for my many friends. Some listen. Some offer a welcome distraction by proposing a fun outing. Some bring by food. Some sit quietly with me. I thank you, Lord, for all the ways they help, big and small. Please let me be such a friend to them!

SEPTEMBER 16

"

I have shewed you all things, how that so labouring ye ought to support the weak.

—EXODUS 20:25

HOW glad I am that we have tools to help us work! Even a tool as simple as a hammer or a screwdriver can make a job easier. Thank you, Lord, for giving us the tools we need to do our jobs. Help us to be tools as well and to make others lives easier through our assistance.

SEPTEMBER 17

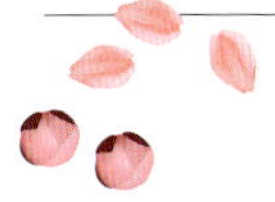

"

When I consider thy heavens, the work of thy fingers, the moon and the stars, which thou hast ordained; What is man, that thou art mindful of him? and the son of man, that thou visitest him?

—PSALM 8:3–4

LORD, thank you for wildlife sanctuaries, the open range, prairies, and mountains; for backyard gardens; for corn stalks and bean stems growing tall then bending low for harvest; and for your generous gifts that meet human need. Lord of all, to you we raise our hymn of grateful praise.

SEPTEMBER 18

“

Sing unto the Lord with thanksgiving; sing praise upon the harp unto our God.

—PSALM 147:7

LORD, I don't have a harp, but I do have a grateful heart. I want to sing praise unto you with thanksgiving today. I might not make a noise, but my heart is grateful, and your goodness fills my thoughts.

SEPTEMBER 19

"

Being enriched in every thing to all bountifulness, which causeth through us thanksgiving to God.

—2 CORINTHIANS 9:11

WHEN I am thankful for what I have, I am given more. When I am not thankful, what I have is taken away. Gratitude is like a door that, when opened, leads to even more good things. But to be ungrateful keeps that door closed, and keeps me away from what God wants to bless me with. I am thankful, always.

SEPTEMBER 20

The prayer of faith shall save the sick, and the Lord shall raise him up.

—JAMES 5:15

LORD, thank you for bringing others into our lives to help us heal. We appreciate how much they aid us. Please remind us to thank them for reaching out to us. Thank you for extending your love to us through them. Amen.

SEPTEMBER 21

Enter into his gates with thanksgiving, and into his courts with praise: be thankful unto him, and bless his name.

—PSALM 100:4

VISUALIZE going to church. As you enter the building, you begin to thank God for his kindness to you. Then you enter the lobby, or the "courts," and your heart is even more full of gratitude. You can begin your day the same way for God is present with you always. Give thanks for his love.

SEPTEMBER 22

"

This poor man cried, and the Lord heard him, and saved him out of all his troubles. The angel of the Lord encampeth round about them that fear him, and delivereth them.

—*PSALM 34:6–7*

CERTAIN days, certain events come bounding into our way to remind us of how out of control life really is. It is then that we are most grateful for the angels that guard our way and guide our paths.

SEPTEMBER 23

Jesus said unto him, Thou shalt love the Lord thy God with all thy heart, and with all thy soul, and with all thy mind.

—MATTHEW 22:37

LORD, I want my love for you to be expressed as naturally as breathing in and out. In that way my whole existence will be an expression of my love for you. Accept my meager attempts to love you completely, Lord.

SEPTEMBER 24

"

For by him were all things created, that are in heaven, and that are in earth, visible and invisible, whether they be thrones, or dominions, or principalities, or powers: all things were created by him, and for him.

—COLOSSIANS 1:16

CREATION shouts to me, Lord, about how amazing you are. I see the wonder of your wisdom in everything from the solar system to how bodies of water feed into one another to the life cycles of all living creatures. Everywhere I turn there is something that makes me think about how creative and insightful you are. Thank you for this universe that speaks without words. I hear it loud and clear, and it tells me of your magnificence.

SEPTEMBER 25

"

Jesus stood and cried, saying, If any man thirst, let him come unto me, and drink. He that believeth on me, as the scripture hath said, out of his belly shall flow rivers of living water.

—JOHN 7:37–38

INSPIRED by you, God, and grateful for the unique gifts we're discovering, we toss ourselves into the stream of life to make ripples wherever we are. In your hands, our gifts can offer a gift that keeps on making ever-widening circles to reach all those stranded on shore.

SEPTEMBER 26

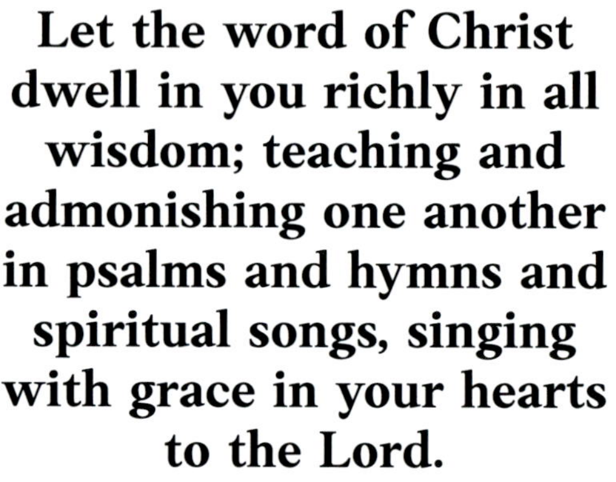

"Let the word of Christ dwell in you richly in all wisdom; teaching and admonishing one another in psalms and hymns and spiritual songs, singing with grace in your hearts to the Lord.

—COLOSSIANS 3:16

THANK you, Lord, for teachers. How can I ever repay the men and women who taught me and opened my eyes to the world? How can I ever truly thank the people who teach my children and guide them on their journey through life? I am so grateful for those who teach and mentor. Thank you for giving us knowledge and wisdom to carry on life's path.

SEPTEMBER 27

Giving thanks always for all things unto God and the Father in the name of our Lord Jesus Christ.

—EPHESIANS 5:20

YOU can always give thanks for all things in the name of Christ. You can say Christ is in control, and he is gracious and merciful. You can give thanks for that which is pleasant and that which is hard. Gratitude can be a source of inner strength.

SEPTEMBER 28

But let all those that put their trust in thee rejoice: let them ever shout for joy, because thou defendest them: let them also that love thy name be joyful in thee.

—PSALM 5:11

TOO often we hop in our cars or take the bus or train without thinking about how much these ways of transportation make our lives easier. I am grateful for transportation that helps me reach my destinations more quickly. How wonderful it is to get somewhere in just a few minutes or be able to visit someone who lives far away! With every bump of the wheels, may I be grateful for the machines that take me where I need to go.

SEPTEMBER 29

"

For God hath not given us the spirit of fear; but of power, and of love, and of a sound mind.

—2 TIMOTHY 1:7

FATHER, I pray today for a clear path, a strong wind at my back pushing me forward, and the courage of a lion to step into greatness. I am afraid and uncomfortable, but with you I can begin the journey of a thousand miles—with one bold step.

SEPTEMBER 30

"Let the heavens rejoice, and let the earth be glad; let the sea roar, and the fulness thereof. Let the field be joyful, and all that is therein: then shall all the trees of the wood rejoice.

—PSALM 96:11–12

LORD, the intricacies of your creation are amazing! We appreciate the glorious fall colors, the radiant sunsets, and the starlit nights. We watch the animal world in awe of the design of each creature. Everything you made is excellent, Lord. May we never take any part of your creation for granted.

Daily Gratitude

OCTOBER

OCTOBER 1

And the fruit of righteousness is sown in peace of them that make peace.

—JAMES 3:18

THIS is the time of year when we like stews and soups and chili, meals prepared in the slow cooker, where our house smells warm and cozy. Thank you, Lord, for the blessings of this time of year, for warm drinks on crisp days, for the memories of picking apples, and for all the comforts we enjoy around us.

OCTOBER 2

There is a friend that sticketh closer than a brother.

—PROVERBS 18:24

LORD, please shine through me and help me lighten another's darkness by showing the same friendship that you extended. Show me a person that is in desperate need of a friend today. Help me to be sensitive, caring, and willing to go out of my way to meet this person's need right now, whether it be emotional, physical, or spiritual. Thank you that when I need a friend, you are the friend that sticketh closer than a brother.

OCTOBER 3

As we have therefore opportunity, let us do good unto all men, especially unto them who are of the household of faith.

—*GALATIANS 6:10*

THANK you, God, for my life. Today I realize I have so much to be thankful for. My life may not be perfect, but nevertheless it is full of good things, beauty, and many wonders. Thank you, Lord, for everything you have given me and the opportunities I've had. Please make me aware of all I have to celebrate and appreciate.

OCTOBER 4

My heart is inditing a good matter: I speak of the things which I have made touching the king: my tongue is the pen of a ready writer.

—PSALM 45:1

THANK you for the gift of writing. What a joy it is to express myself through words! A letter, a diary entry, a blog, or a report—all these things are ways I can share my thoughts and knowledge with the world. I am grateful for the chance to express myself and pray that God will guide my pen every time I write.

OCTOBER 5

"

O Lord, how manifold are thy works! in wisdom hast thou made them all: the earth is full of thy riches. So is this great and wide sea, wherein are things creeping innumerable, both small and great beasts.

—PSALM 104:24–25

LORD, today I feel particularly grateful for pets. What joy and companionship animals bring us each day. I know you created them, and I can see a bit of your majesty in them. Thank you for populating our world with such lovable creatures.

OCTOBER 6

Naked came I out of my mother's womb, and naked shall I return thither: the Lord gave, and the Lord hath taken away; blessed be the name of the Lord.

—JOB 1:21

YOU didn't bring much to this life, and you will take away nothing. But the Lord has given you family, friends, strength, and joy. He has given you the breath of life. Blessed be his name.

OCTOBER 7

"

Behold, I will do a new thing; now it shall spring forth; shall ye not know it? I will even make a way in the wilderness, and rivers in the desert.

—ISAIAH 43:19

LORD, sometimes I think back to who I was before I knew you, and I don't even recognize myself. That's how great the change is when you make us new creations! I'm so glad that the person I was isn't nearly as important in your eyes as the person you know I can be. I may have been younger and fitter then, but I was lost on this worldly adventure. Thank you, Lord, for claiming me as your own and making everything new in my life!

OCTOBER 8

The disciple is not above his master: but every one that is perfect shall be as his master.

—LUKE 6:40

I went out recently at a time when the roads were filled with school buses. As I watched the children get on the buses that take them to school, I felt thankful for my own school days. Thank you, Lord, for my education and the doors it has opened for me. Thank you for the friends I made, the lessons I learned, and the teachers who guided me and helped me find my place in the world.

The Lord shall preserve thy going out and thy coming in from this time forth, and even for evermore.

—PSALM 121:8

DEAR God, thank you for the opportunity to adventure. Please bless my travels. Please guide and protect me as I visit new places, meet new people, and broaden my horizons. May I make the most of my journey.

OCTOBER 10

And the world passeth away, and the lust thereof: but he that doeth the will of God abideth for ever.

—1 JOHN 2:17

LORD, help me to relax and enjoy time instead of feeling like it is my enemy. Help me be grateful for each minute and the special joys it brings. Sometimes I need to slow down and think of time as my friend. Thank you, Lord, for time and the gifts it brings me.

OCTOBER 11

“

Remove far from me vanity and lies: give me neither poverty nor riches; feed me with food convenient for me.

—PROVERBS 30:8

LORD, as I struggle to balance my budget, I ask myself: What is wealth? Is it having material riches, plenty of food, clothing, a house, and freedom from worry about money? You have taught me, Father, that it is none of these things. True wealth is having work to do. It is being cared for by a loving God. It is enjoying the love of friends and family. You give me all I need or want, Lord.

OCTOBER 12

❝

Let all bitterness, and wrath, and anger, and clamour, and evil speaking, be put away from you, with all malice.

—EPHESIANS 4:31

SOME time ago, a friend drifted away. She became busy with new commitments and had less and less time for our friendship. After a while, I stopped trying to maintain the friendship by myself. When I look back and feel resentful or rejected, please help me to feel grateful instead. While it wasn't a lifelong friendship, it was a good one while it lasted. I ask you to bless her today and all her endeavors.

OCTOBER 13

Oh how great is thy goodness, which thou hast laid up for them that fear thee; which thou hast wrought for them that trust in thee before the sons of men!

—*PSALM 31:19*

HOW great is your goodness, Lord. You have laid it up for me, layer upon layer. You have shown me your kindness over and over again. Today I ask that you help me to fear and trust you—and to be grateful.

OCTOBER 14

Wondrous God, I praise your name.
Your Word is life.
I believe you can heal me.
Be with me when I am sick,
And remind me to praise you
Once I am well again.
Thank you for healing me in the past
And for future healing.
Keep me in good health
That I might serve you
And praise your name.
Amen.

OCTOBER 15

"

**Beareth all things,
believeth all things,
hopeth all things,
endureth all things.**

—1 CORINTHIANS 13:7

LORD, how grateful I am to have found the love of my life. May I never take my spouse for granted. May I focus on our strengths and be quick to forget any silly disagreements. Help me to be an encourager and friend as well as a lover. Protect the bond between us, Lord. Keep it strong, healthy, and loving.

OCTOBER 16

And after the earthquake a fire; but the Lord was not in the fire: and after the fire a still small voice.

—1 KINGS 19:12

LORD, help me hear that "still small voice" in the world. So often I am surrounded by the noise of others and the noise I make myself. Thank you for reminding me to listen to the small sounds and see your glory in little things. Help me listen and hear you in the whispers of the world.

OCTOBER 17

And when the Lord saw her, he had compassion on her, and said unto her, Weep not. And he came and touched the bier: and they that bare him stood still. And he said, Young man, I say unto thee, Arise.

—LUKE 7:13–14

THE widow whose only son died didn't even need to ask Jesus for help. When he saw her desperate grief, he reached out to perform a miracle. I can only imagine her incredulous joy, and how startled and amazed all the mourners must have been. Those who were bearing the bier must have seen something in this stranger who came to them, that they halted when Jesus came close. May I be so attuned to your presence, Jesus, that I stop to allow you to work. I thank you, Jesus, for the unexpected gifts you have given me.

OCTOBER 18

I will greatly rejoice in the Lord, my soul shall be joyful in my God.

—ISAIAH 61:10

WHAT a joyful noise is the sound of children playing! Thank you for the chance to play with my children, to be silly with them, and to enter their world and share their zest for life. Thank you for allowing me to be young again as I share their joy and their imagination. Thank you for the gift of having a child's joy.

OCTOBER 19

"

Let him that stole steal no more: but rather let him labour, working with his hands the thing which is good, that he may have to give to him that needeth.

—EPHESIANS 4:28

I thank you for my work, Lord. And please bless me in it. Most of all, help me to remember that the paycheck worth working for consists of more than just money. It must include meaning and significance, for myself and others.

OCTOBER 20

In every thing give thanks: for this is the will of God in Christ Jesus concerning you.

—1 THESSALONIANS 5:18

LORD, I have to admit the "everything" here is hard. Sometimes my fear keeps me from seeing what good you have in mind. Help me to trust you, Lord, even when I don't quite understand. And help me to give thanks.

OCTOBER 21

"

Praise ye the Lord. I will praise the Lord with my whole heart, in the assembly of the upright, and in the congregation.

—PSALM 111:1

I am grateful for my church, Father. I love to be with your people, praising you. Help me to do it with my whole heart, joining a chorus of grateful voices. You are our God, and we praise you.

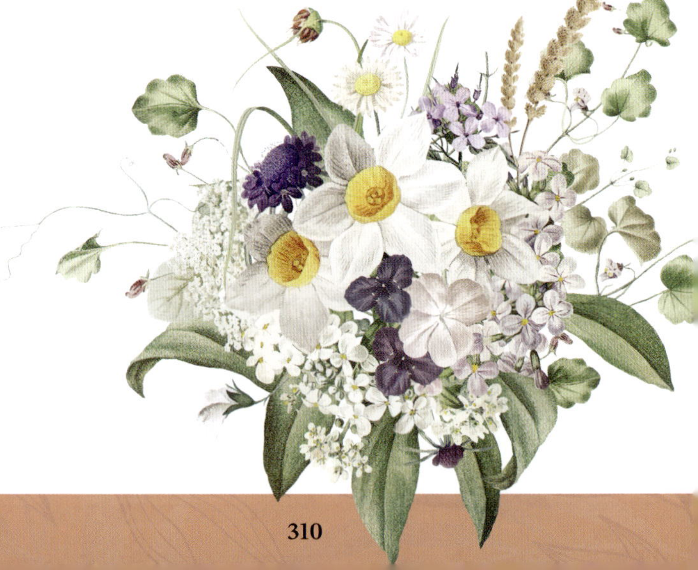

OCTOBER 22

"And he shall be as the light of the morning, when the sun riseth, even a morning without clouds; as the tender grass springing out of the earth by clear shining after rain.

—2 SAMUEL 23:4

LORD, how grateful I am that you are willing to go before me to prepare the way. Even when I sense that a new opportunity is from you and has your blessing, I've learned I still need to stop and ask you to lead before I take the first step. Otherwise I will stumble along in the dark tripping over stones of my own creation! Everything goes more smoothly when you are involved, Lord.

OCTOBER 23

"

Yea, the Lord shall give that which is good; and our land shall yield her increase.

—PSALM 85:12

FALL is a time of change. Sometimes that change is beautiful, as when the leaves begin to change color. Sometimes that change brings loss, as the days grow shorter and the trees grow bare. Let me never be afraid to change and grow myself—and let me remember that you are with me even in times of loss and sorrow.

OCTOBER 24

The meek will he guide in judgment: and the meek will he teach his way.

—PSALM 25:9

I will tell you, I have heard . . . God has two dwellings, one in heaven and the other in the meek and thankful heart.

—Izaak Walton

OCTOBER 25

Nay but, O man, who art thou that repliest against God? Shall the thing formed say to him that formed it, Why hast thou made me thus?

—ROMANS 9:20

WHEN things go wrong, God is usually the first we blame. Forgive us for even considering that you would deliberately hurt one of your very own children. For what could you possibly have to gain? Thank you for your presence; forgive our easy blame of you.

OCTOBER 26

When I said, My foot slippeth; thy mercy, O Lord, held me up.

—PSALM 94:18

MY guard is constant and vigilant, protecting me against the next episode of my humanness. I know to err is human, but why so often? Peace only comes, God of wholeness, through reassurance that with you, mistakes, errors, and even disasters can yield treasures. I am so grateful.

OCTOBER 27

O Lord, our Lord, how excellent is thy name in all the earth! who hast set thy glory above the heavens.

—PSALM 8:1

LORD, I am thankful every day that you sent your Son to live among us. How blessed we are that he taught us about you and gave us such a beautiful example to follow. May I remember every day to pause and give thanks for this, so I do not get too caught up in my trivial, worldly cares.

OCTOBER 28

Finally, be ye all of one mind, having compassion one of another, love as brethren, be pitiful, be courteous.

—1 PETER 3:8

TODAY I will find a way to share my gifts with others. It might be something small, but I want to find a way to give something of myself. Thank you, Lord, for being able to share our gifts and for being givers. Even a small gift is a blessing, and I am grateful to both give and receive.

OCTOBER 29

I will worship toward thy holy temple, and praise thy name for thy lovingkindness and for thy truth.

—PSALM 138:2

PRAISE is the essence of worship. Songs are only one way to express our gratitude for God's loving-kindness and truth. Whenever you praise him, you worship him, even if you can't carry a tune.

OCTOBER 30

Now when Daniel knew that the writing was signed, he went into his house; and his windows being open in his chamber toward Jerusalem, he kneeled upon his knees three times a day, and prayed, and gave thanks before his God, as he did aforetime.

—DANIEL 6:10

DANIEL was in a tough place, surrounded by enemies at court and facing legal complications for exercising his faith. What did he do? He prayed and thanked God, just like he always had. Are you in a tough place? Then take inspiration from Daniel and do the same.

OCTOBER 31

Ye are all the children of light, and the children of the day: we are not of the night, nor of darkness.

—1 THESSALONIANS 5:5

HAPPY Halloween! Even though Halloween is built around fear, it can also be a time of joy and gratitude. Thank you for the joy I feel when I see children dressed in costume and enjoying their special night. Thank you for a day when everyone can be as weird as they want to be. Thank you for letting us celebrate the unusual and see the world in a different way.

Daily Gratitude

NOVEMBER

NOVEMBER 1

Blessed are they that mourn: for they shall be comforted.

—*MATTHEW 5:4*

WHEN we grieve for lost loved ones, we grieve for ourselves. Let us celebrate that those who have gone home to heaven now know the full essence of God's true love.

NOVEMBER 2

“

My sheep hear my voice, and I know them, and they follow me: And I give unto them eternal life; and they shall never perish, neither shall any man pluck them out of my hand. My Father, which gave them me, is greater than all; and no man is able to pluck them out of my Father’s hand.

—JOHN 10:27–29

WE praise you, Lord, for eternal life. And we thank you for your love for each one of us. Amen.

NOVEMBER 3

❝

Wherefore, my beloved brethren, let every man be swift to hear, slow to speak, slow to wrath.

—*JAMES 1:19*

LORD, please forgive us in our impatient moments and nudge us back onto the right path. We live in a society that knows nothing of delayed gratification; we often get caught up in the expectation that everything we need from you and ask of you will happen immediately. But we know from experience that your timing is always perfect, Lord. We are blessed and privileged to have time for reflection and growth.

NOVEMBER 4

Provoke not your children to wrath: but bring them up in the nurture and admonition of the Lord.

—EPHESIANS 6:4

THANK you, God, that even when I fret, I know without a doubt you are using my unique gifts and talents to nurture and teach my children. When I get down on myself and am unsure of my abilities, please remind me that your commitment to me is lifelong.

NOVEMBER 5

But God commendeth his love toward us, in that, while we were yet sinners, Christ died for us.

—*ROMANS 5:8*

I am grateful for differences. How boring it would be if every person was the same! How thankful I am not to live in a world full of clones. It's easy to judge people who are different from me, but it is those differences that make the world a wonderful, exciting, and interesting place! Thank you, Lord, for making each person unique, and please help me to be proud of my own uniqueness.

NOVEMBER 6

"

Thine, O Lord is the greatness, and the power, and the glory, and the victory, and the majesty: for all that is in the heaven and in the earth is thine; thine is the kingdom, O Lord, and thou art exalted as head above all.

—1 CHRONICLES 29:11

LORD God, you are everything I have or need. Help me rest is this truth today, for your strength and glory are sufficient for any trial I face or need I have. You alone, Lord, are great and glorious and good.

"

Many, O Lord my God, are thy wonderful works which thou hast done, and thy thoughts which are to us-ward: they cannot be reckoned up in order unto thee: if I would declare and speak of them, they are more than can be numbered.

—*PSALM 40:5*

FATHER, you help us to live gracefully by blessing us with many wonderful friends. Thank you for making them as good as you are.

NOVEMBER 8

There are many devices in a man's heart; nevertheless the counsel of the Lord, that shall stand.

—PROVERBS 19:21

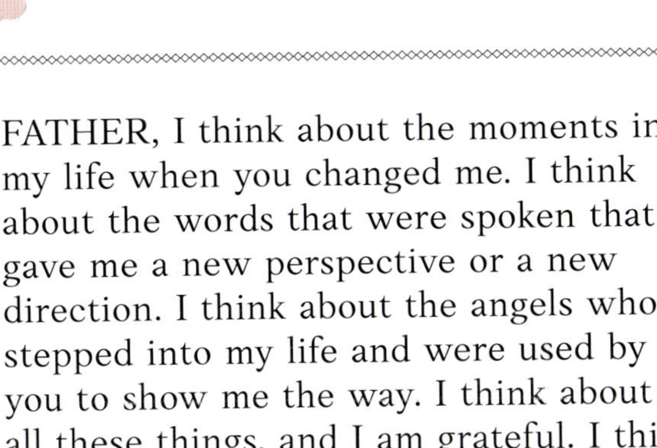

FATHER, I think about the moments in my life when you changed me. I think about the words that were spoken that gave me a new perspective or a new direction. I think about the angels who stepped into my life and were used by you to show me the way. I think about all these things, and I am grateful. I think about all these words and moments, and I am filled with confidence that you have led me on my way.

NOVEMBER 9

“For if ye forgive men their trespasses, your heavenly Father will also forgive you.

—*MATTHEW* 6:14

IN thankfulness for present mercy, nothing so becomes us as losing sight of past ills.

—Lew Wallace

NOVEMBER 10

"

For how great is his goodness, and how great is his beauty! corn shall make the young men cheerful, and new wine the maids.

—ZECHARIAH 9:17

THINK of some simple pleasure or delight—a cup of tea with a friend or a treasured memory from childhood. It is merely a shadow of God's grace. Give thanks for the delight and our God who provides it.

NOVEMBER 11

"

Greater love hath no man than this, that a man lay down his life for his friends.

—JOHN 15:13

THANK you for our veterans and those who serve in the military. May I always remember those who have given up their day-to-day lives just to keep me and my country safe and secure. Help me to show my gratitude toward the veterans I meet and always remember to honor their sacrifices.

NOVEMBER 12

Remember the days of old, consider the years of many generations: ask thy father, and he will shew thee; thy elders, and they will tell thee.

—DEUTERONOMY 32:7

LORD, you have told us to "remember the days of old." As we remember those who have gone before us, we teach our children love and respect for life itself. In giving honor to others, we thank and honor you, O God, for your love and for the great sacrifice of your son, Jesus Christ.

NOVEMBER 13

Whatsoever ye do, do it heartily, as to the Lord.

—COLOSSIANS 3:23

THANK you for employment. I may not enjoy all aspects of my job, but I'm grateful for the financial security it offers. I'm grateful for the dignity of work, for my conscientious colleagues, and for those days when I feel like I'm getting to use my God-given talents fully! I ask for your blessings today on those looking for employment, that you give them a spirit of hope and patience as they wait for the right work to come along.

NOVEMBER 14

"

We praise thy mighty, great God of right,
We praise thy pow'r and majesty;
We praise thy love, that from above,
Sends down its blessing ceaselessly.

In grateful praise, Lord, all our days,
Our songs shall rise unto the throne;
Grant when, at last, the goal is passed,
We may be gathered with thine own.

—William Henry Gardner

NOVEMBER 15

“

If we live in the Spirit, let us also walk in the Spirit.

—*GALATIANS 5:25*

LORD, remind us of a childhood memory of someone in uniform who made a difference in our lives: a school nurse who comforted us, a firefighter who spoke to us on a field trip to the local station, a police officer standing on the neighborhood corner, or a doctor who treated us for a childhood illness. Thank you for showing us that someone in uniform could be trusted and could be a friend.

NOVEMBER 16

Therefore if any man be in Christ, he is a new creature: old things are passed away; behold, all things are become new.

—2 CORINTHIANS 5:17

THE creative power within is your power to overcome any obstacle and break through any binding walls that keep you from your dreams. This power was given to you by the greatest of all creators, the one who created you, God. Just look around at the amazing beauty and diversity of the world you live in, and you will never again doubt that God supports your creative endeavors.

NOVEMBER 17

For the Lord God is a sun and shield: the Lord will give grace and glory: no good thing will he withhold from them that walk uprightly.

—PSALM 84:11

LORD, you are my sun and my shield. You are the source of my strength and the light of my days. You protect me and provide for me. Every good thing is from you. Thank you, Father, for your grace.

NOVEMBER 18

“

A time to weep, and a time to laugh; a time to mourn, and a time to dance.

—ECCLESIASTES 3:4

THANK you, Lord, for reddened eyes. Believing your promise that comfort follows mourning, we bawl and sob. In your wisdom, onion-peeling salty tears differ from cleansing grieving ones; we’re grateful for their healing. Deliver us from stiff upper lips, and if we’ve lost our tears, help us find them.

NOVEMBER 19

For the kingdom of God is not meat and drink; but righteousness, and peace, and joy in the Holy Ghost.

—*ROMANS 14:17*

THERE is no denying the pleasure of creature comforts. Thank you, God, for all the technology and advancements that make my home and life more comfortable. It is good to feel good! But may I always be cognizant of well-being on the inside as well as the outside; may my focus on the everlasting rewards of your kingdom be unwavering.

NOVEMBER 20

"

My little children, let us not love in word, neither in tongue; but in deed and in truth.

—1 JOHN 3:18

LORD, even when I'm tired and have too much to do, give me your spirit of graciousness during the coming holiday season. Allow me to open my heart to all those I encounter and to treat each visitor to my home as an honored guest. Most of all, let me be hospitable without regard to whether the person will ever return the favor. I want to greet everyone as you would greet them, Lord, with compassion and an unconditional welcome.

NOVEMBER 21

Wherefore I also, after I heard of your faith in the Lord Jesus, and love unto all the saints, Cease not to give thanks for you, making mention of you in my prayers.

—EPHESIANS 1:15–16

WHEN we give thanks and praise to someone, we honor the presence of God in that person. Our gratitude for the people we love is our acknowledgment of spirit expressing through them. In all situations, let us express our gratitude to God.

NOVEMBER 22

I will praise thee: for thou hast heard me, and art become my salvation.

—PSALM 118:21

FATHER God, thank you for hearing me. I am grateful that when I am discouraged or overwhelmed, you listen to me and save me. I am comforted daily by your presence. I will fill my thoughts with gratitude for you today.

NOVEMBER 23

"

Unto thee, O God, do we give thanks, unto thee do we give thanks: for that thy name is near thy wondrous works declare.

—PSALM 75:1

AS you look around, you see God's wondrous works. You see them in the faces of those you love and in the changing majesty of the clouds. You see them in the breaking sunrise and the delight of children. Give thanks to God for all the beauty in this world and the heavens above.

NOVEMBER 24

What shall I render unto the Lord for all his benefits toward me?

—PSALM 116:12

COUNT your blessings and see how they multiply! Every challenge teaches us something we need to know. Every obstacle gives us more strength. Every problem gives us a chance to stretch our minds and come up with a new solution. All the lessons—good or bad—add up to an abundance of blessings we can choose to appreciate.

NOVEMBER 25

But to do good and to communicate forget not: for with such sacrifices God is well pleased.

—HEBREWS 13:16

THANK you, God, for letting us know you exist through families and friends who feed us more than enough food, who give us abundant shelter and clothing, and who cherish your presence and honor your creation. Lord of all, to you we raise our hymn of grateful praise.

NOVEMBER 26

For unto us a child is born, unto us a son is given: and the government shall be upon his shoulder: and his name shall be called Wonderful, Counsellor, The mighty God, The everlasting Father, The Prince of Peace.

—ISAIAH 9:6

JESUS, you are at once awe-inspiring and a friend. Your words bring both challenging truth and peaceful comfort. As I look forward to your birth this advent, I think of the innocent baby born in a manger, the man who died for us, and the miracle of your resurrection.

NOVEMBER 27

But let it be the hidden man of the heart, in that which is not corruptible, even the ornament of a meek and quiet spirit, which is in the sight of God of great price.

—1 PETER 3:4

LITTLE changes become apparent from year to year in this life. Maybe there's an extra pound or two on our frame. Maybe we've spotted a new gray hair—or two or twenty. Perhaps we suddenly realize we're taking things a bit more slowly. As our bodies begin to show signs of age, our inner self grows in radiance, compounding in beauty, flourishing in faith. We are just beginning to blossom within and display the brightness that will burst forth in heaven when our life is finally fully opened to the light of God's love.

NOVEMBER 28

"Is any sick among you? let him call for the elders of the church; and let them pray over him, anointing him with oil in the name of the Lord.

—JAMES 5:14

MEDICINE is such a great gift! I wonder what the wise men and women in olden times would think of the medicines we have today. Thank you, Lord, for giving doctors and scientists the desire and the wisdom to create medicines that help so many people every day. Thank you for their work making my life easier and for making what was once impossible very possible today.

NOVEMBER 29

And I have filled him with the spirit of God, in wisdom, and in understanding, and in knowledge, and in all manner of workmanship, To devise cunning works, to work in gold, and in silver, and in brass, And in cutting of stones, to set them, and in carving of timber, to work in all manner of workmanship.

—EXODUS 31:3–5

HOW excited I am when I get a new phone or computer! I am so grateful for how these tools improve my life. Technology helps me stay in touch with people who are far away and share news in an instant. I am grateful for the way technology has made the world a smaller place, how it helps keeps people together, and makes work easier.

NOVEMBER 30

"

For I am persuaded, that neither death, nor life, nor angels, nor principalities, nor powers, nor things present, nor things to come, Nor height, nor depth, nor any other creature, shall be able to separate us from the love of God, which is in Christ Jesus our Lord.

—ROMANS 8:38–39

LORD, love indeed makes the world go around and nothing compares to your love. My prayers today are not just for myself, but for all living things, that we may all feel a little more loved and cherished. So many of us go through life thinking we don't matter. I pray your love awakens others to truly understand, as I do, that every life is precious in your sight. Love is the greatest miracle, Lord, and I am grateful to experience your love daily.

Daily Gratitude

DECEMBER

DECEMBER 1

"

Now I praise you, brethren, that ye remember me in all things, and keep the ordinances, as I delivered them to you.

—1 CORINTHIANS 11:2

TAKING part in family traditions is such a joyous experience! Today I will take time to recall the traditions I experienced as a child and the family times I shared with those around me. I am grateful for those memories and for the opportunity to share those traditions with my family and friends today. Continuing a tradition feels like taking joyful steps along a path from the past to the future.

DECEMBER 2

Whether therefore ye eat, or drink, or whatsoever ye do, do all to the glory of God.

—1 CORINTHIANS 10:31

EVERY bite you eat today and every task you do is a reason to thank God. Thank him for the opportunity. Thank him for the strength. Thank him for the resources. In this way, you give him glory and praise.

DECEMBER 3

“

For I know the thoughts that I think toward you, saith the Lord, thoughts of peace, and not of evil, to give you an expected end.

—JEREMIAH 29:11

God, thank you for sometimes reminding me that in the center of chaos lies the seed of new opportunity and that things are not always as awful as they seem at first. I often forget that what starts out bad can end up great and that it is all a matter of my own perspective.

DECEMBER 4

"

And in that day thou shalt say, O Lord, I will praise thee: though thou wast angry with me, thine anger is turned away, and thou comfortedst me.

—ISAIAH 12:1

LORD, I have failed you in so many ways, but I will summon my inner strength today to examine how I can do better in the future. There are times when I have acted out of anger when I could have been kind. I have leaned into bitterness when I would have been better served by tempering my thoughts with sweetness. Thank you for your patience with me. Please help to make me more like you.

DECEMBER 5

Iron sharpeneth iron; so a man sharpeneth the countenance of his friend.

—PROVERBS 27:17

WHAT a gift friendship is! I am grateful for my friends. Some friends have known me for many years. We grew up together and watched each other change and grow. Other friends are newer but no less dear. Thank you, Lord, for all the friends you have placed in my life and for the memories we have created together.

DECEMBER 6

Blessed are your eyes, for they see: and your ears, for they hear.

—MATTHEW 13:16

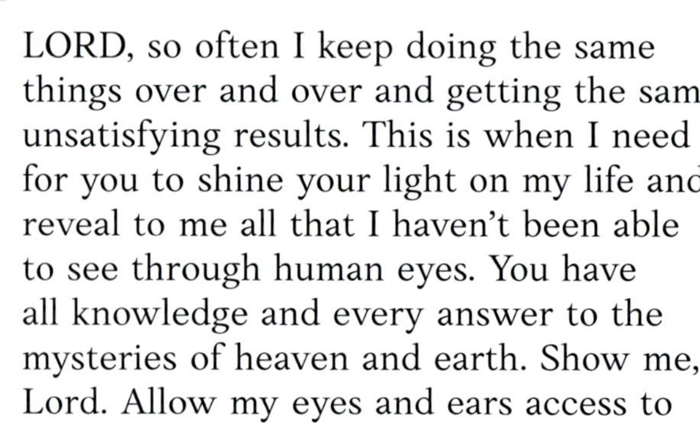

LORD, so often I keep doing the same things over and over and getting the same unsatisfying results. This is when I need for you to shine your light on my life and reveal to me all that I haven't been able to see through human eyes. You have all knowledge and every answer to the mysteries of heaven and earth. Show me, Lord. Allow my eyes and ears access to a bit more of the knowledge you possess, and thank you for your patience.

DECEMBER 7

The Lord God took the man, and put him into the garden of Eden to dress it and to keep it.

—GENESIS 2:15

YOU invented work, God, and I am grateful. Thank you for the important projects you've given me. Help me, Lord of Creation, pause to look after the details, and please accomplish your masterwork in my soul this day.

DECEMBER 8

I will praise thee, O Lord my God, with all my heart: and I will glorify thy name for evermore.

—PSALM 86:12

LORD, there are few things I do with all my heart, but let my gratitude be one of them. Fill me every day with sincere and simple praise for who you are and what you do. I know my humble appreciation for your works is enough to bring me closer to you.

DECEMBER 9

Let the beauty of the Lord our God be upon us: and establish thou the work of our hands upon us; yea, the work of our hands establish thou it.

—PSALM 90:17

WE spend so much time shopping and decorating! It seems small, but God, please do help me choose good gifts for my family and friends, thoughtful ones that express my love for them. But please also don't let my ego get wrapped up in it, forgetting that the connection we share is more important than any individual gift. Let me stay focused on love this season, as always: your love for us, our love for you, and our love for each other.

DECEMBER 10

The heaven, even the heavens, are the Lord's: but the earth hath he given to the children of men.

—PSALM 115:16

EVERY day is a journey through time and space. Thank you, Lord, for the journeys that make up my life and take me to amazing places. I am grateful for the things I've learned on my life's journey. Allow me to appreciate the journey more than the destination and keep an open mind for the unexpected gifts on the road. I may not always end up where I thought I would, but I am grateful for the paths I travel!

DECEMBER 11

Give unto the Lord the glory due unto his name; worship the Lord in the beauty of holiness.

—*PSALM 29:2*

IT can be hard to praise God as much as he deserves, but we can try. His holiness is so beautiful we can do nothing less than give thanks. Worship him throughout the day, and feel how your joyous gratitude for God lightens your step.

DECEMBER 12

Yet I will rejoice in the Lord, I will joy in the God of my salvation.

—HABAKKUK 3:18

YET I will rejoice. When the car doesn't start or my job challenges me, yet I will rejoice. When my spouse is rude or my child seems distant, yet I will rejoice. I will take joy in the God of my salvation and trust him to make all things right.

DECEMBER 13

Watch ye, stand fast in the faith, quit you like men, be strong.

—1 CORINTHIANS 16:13

LIKE a toddler who falls more than he stands, I'm pulling myself upright in the aftermath of death. I know you as a companion, God of mending hearts, and feel you steadying me. Thank you for the gift of resilience. Lead me to others who have hurt and gone on; I need to see how it's done and find courage through faith.

DECEMBER 14

To every thing there is a season, and a time to every purpose under the heaven.

—ECCLESIASTES 3:1

THE past does not have to be an enemy. Rather let it be a friend and an ally that reminds you of where you've been, how far you've come, and what you've learned along the way. Then let it go as you would a favorite but little-used old garment, with love and gratitude, knowing that God will always provide you with something wonderful and new to wear along the way.

DECEMBER 15

He that is slow to wrath is of great understanding: but he that is hasty of spirit exalteth folly.

—PROVERBS 14:29

WHY am I so contrary? I wonder and worry. Perhaps it is tiredness, frustration, or pressure, but too often I lose my cool and then the children do likewise until we make even more problems. I'm so grateful that God can help us repair and reset.

DECEMBER 16

Every moving thing that liveth shall be meat for you; even as the green herb have I given you all things.

—GENESIS 9:3

WHEN I go to the supermarket, I am amazed at all the food I find there! As I walk down the store aisles, gratitude fills me for everyone who makes food available to me. I give thanks to the farmers and manufacturers, to those who grow the food and those who package and transport it to me. May I always appreciate their hard work and the bounty they produce.

DECEMBER 17

Not that I speak in respect of want: for I have learned, in whatsoever state I am, therewith to be content.

—PHILIPPIANS 4:11

GOD, you have graced our home with your love. We may not have granite countertops in our kitchen, and the bathrooms, while bright and clean, have outdated fixtures. But I look around our little house each day and feel joy. May I not allow materialism to distract me or create anxiety; may I be grateful for the true blessings in my life.

Bless the Lord, O my soul, and all that is within me, bless his holy name.

—PSALM 103:1

HELP me, Lord, to praise you with every fiber of my being, with all that is within me. You are faithful, gracious, and holy. You are my God; my hope is in you.

DECEMBER 19

The heart of the prudent getteth knowledge; and the ear of the wise seeketh knowledge.

—PROVERBS 18:15

WHAT a wonderful gift a book is! Thank you, Lord, for the gift of books, for words and poetry and stories. When I pick up a good book, I am taken away to another place and have the chance to discover amazing people. Thank you for the writers who create the books I love and who have invited me into their worlds.

DECEMBER 20

For if they fall, the one will lift up his fellow: but woe to him that is alone when he falleth; for he hath not another to help him up. Again, if two lie together, then they have heat: but how can one be warm alone? And if one prevail against him, two shall withstand him; and a threefold cord is not quickly broken.

—ECCLESIASTES 4:10–12

HEAVENLY Father, I am glad to have even just one companion, but you have sent me many more! I thank you for my friends and family. I am happy to have so many shoulders on which I can lean.

DECEMBER 21

But grow in grace, and in the knowledge of our Lord and Saviour Jesus Christ. To him be glory both now and for ever. Amen.

—2 PETER 3:18

WE can relax, O Lord of light, on this the longest darkness of the year, knowing that in order for trees to blossom and bear fruit and the maple tree to yield its sugar, a resting stillness of dormancy is a welcome part of growth.

DECEMBER 22

Better is a dry morsel, and quietness therewith, than an house full of sacrifices with strife.

—PROVERBS 17:1

LORD, it gets so crowded when everyone's home for the holidays—and there can be strife! It's easy for us to long for a quick return to our quieter day-to-day lives. Don't let our desire for peace and quiet rob us of the joy of spending time with loved ones, Lord! You've blessed us with quiet times and celebratory times, and we want to make the most of both.

DECEMBER 23

"

Lord Jesus Christ, our Lord most dear,
as thou wast once an infant here,
so give this child of thine, we pray,
thy grace and blessing day by day.
O holy Jesus, Lord divine,
we pray thee guard this child of thine.

—Heinrich von Laufenberg,
Trans. Catherine Winkworth

DECEMBER 24

Now the God of peace, that brought again from the dead our Lord Jesus, that great shepherd of the sheep, through the blood of the everlasting covenant, Make you perfect in every good work to do his will, working in you that which is wellpleasing in his sight, through Jesus Christ; to whom be glory for ever and ever. Amen.

—HEBREWS 13:20–21

THE Christmas tree, O God, is groaning beneath gift-wrapped anticipation. The table spread before us is resplendent with shared foods prepared by loving hands, for which we give thanks. And now, as this waiting season ticks to a bell-ringing, midnight-marvelous close, we around this table are scooting over to make room for the anticipated Guest. Come, blessing us with the gift of your presence as we say, "Welcome."

Glory to God in the highest, and on earth peace, good will toward men.

—LUKE 2:14

MERRY Christmas! Thank you, Lord, for this special day. It is the birthday of your son, Jesus, and a bright and beautiful day for the world. Today I am grateful for rebirth, for celebrations, and for sharing traditions with the people I love. Thank you for the gift of joy and new life.

DECEMBER 26

Jesus saith unto him, I am the way, the truth, and the life: no man cometh unto the Father, but by me.

—JOHN 14:6

CHRIST is born, go forth to meet Him,
Christ by all the heaven adored;
Singing songs of welcome, greet Him,
For the earth receives her Lord.
All ye nations, shout and sing;
For He comes, your glorious King.

—Traditional hymn

DECEMBER 27

Thanks be to God, which giveth us the victory through our Lord Jesus Christ.

—1 CORINTHIANS 15:57

LORD, how grateful we are that our spirits don't have to sag once the excitement of Christmas is over! We don't want to be like ungrateful children tearing through a pile of presents just to say, "Is that all?" For the gift you gave us at Christmas, your beloved Son among us, is a gift that is ours all the days of our lives and throughout eternity! Thank you for the greatest gift of all, Lord.

DECEMBER 28

Heaviness in the heart of man maketh it stoop: but a good word maketh it glad.

—PROVERBS 12:25

THE days after Christmas can sometimes be a bit of a letdown, but they can be peaceful too. After all the preparation and rush, we have a little time to reflect and talk. Things that weren't "important" enough to get brought up at the big family meals make their way into conversation. Let me be grateful, Lord, for these gentle times of relaxation and renewal as we prepare for the end of the year.

DECEMBER 29

The height to which love exalts is unspeakable. Love unites us to God. Love covers a multitude of sins. Love beareth all things, is long-suffering in all things. There is nothing base, nothing arrogant in love. By love have all elect of God been made perfect.

—Clement of Rome

DECEMBER 30

The Lord bless thee, and keep thee: The Lord make his face shine upon thee, and be gracious unto thee: The Lord lift up his countenance upon thee, and give thee peace.

—*NUMBERS 6:24–26*

LORD, sometimes it seems as if life is a series of goodbyes. I know when I think this way I am focusing on the wrong part, though—for life can also be a series of hellos! Even when the holidays are over and we go back to our day-to-day lives, we come upon beautiful moments. We just need to be on the lookout and ready to accept them into our lives. May I always be ready to accept blessings from you, Lord, whether they are large blessings that bowl me over or small blessings I may miss if I'm too caught up in my own concerns.

DECEMBER 31

The sufferings of this present time are not worthy to be compared with the glory which shall be revealed in us.

—ROMANS 8:18

WE are closing out the year tonight! Dear Lord, I ask for safety for my family, friends, and all those we love, both tonight as people attend celebrations and drive home, and in the year to come. I ask that I have a clear eye in the coming year to see all the ways in which you bless me abundantly. And I thank you for your love that surrounds me, enfolds me, and heals me. With you at my side, I am never alone.